Military Dress of North America 1665-1970

Military Dress of North America 1665-1970

MARTIN WINDROW & GERRY EMBLETON

CHARLES SCRIBNER'S SONS · NEW YORK

Contents

Printed in Great Britain
Library of Congress Catalog Card Number 73-9486
SBN 684-13551-5 (cloth)

Bibliography

Among the many published works consulted during the preparation of this book, interested readers may find the following of particular value:

Soldiers of the American Army Fritz Kredel & Frederick P. Todd: Chicago, 1950

The Book of the Continental Soldier Harold L. Peterson: Harrisburg, 1968

Uniforms of the American, British, French and German Armies in the War of the American Revolution Charles M. Lefferts: New York, 1926

A Pictorial History of the United States Army Gene Gurney: New York, 1966

A History of the Uniforms of the British Army Cecil C. P. Lawson: London, 1941

American History Atlas Martin Gilbert: London, 1968

Arms and Armor in Colonial America Harold L. Peterson: New York, 1956

History Written With Pick And Shovel Calver & Bolton: New York, 1950

Red Coat and Brown Bess Anthony Darling: London, 1970

Accoutrements of the Army of the United States (1839-61) J. N. Jacobsen: New York, 1968

Civil War Handbook William H. Price: Fairfax, Va.; 1961

Divided We Fought ed David Donald: New York, 1952

Embattled Confederates B. Wiley & H. Milhollen: New York, 1964

They Who Fought Here B. Wiley & H. Milhollen: New York, 1959

Uniforms of the Civil War F. Lord & A. Wise: New York, 1970

Arms and Equipment of the Civil War Jack Coggins: New York, 1962

The Fighting Man Jack Coggins: New York, 1966

Long Knife Glenn Dines: New York, 1961

US Army Headgear to 1854 E. Howell & D. Kloster: Washington D.C., 1969

Handbooks of English Costume (various titles) P. Cunnington: London, 1964

The United States Marines Lynn Montross: New York, 1959

Historical Arms Series (various titles) Museum Restoration Service, Ottawa

Recollections of a Rogue Samuel Chamberlain: London, 1957

Sketch Book 76 R. Klinger & R. Wilder: Arlington, 1967

British Military Uniforms from Contemporary Pictures W. Y. Carman: London, 1957

American Heritage Magazine, various issues

National Geographic Magazine, various issues

Journal of the Society for Army Historical Research, various issues

Foreword

The most difficult choice which has faced us during the preparation of this book has been the selection of a title which conveyed the contents accurately but in less than ponderous detail. It seemed to us to be inappropriate to compile a book on the uniforms worn by the American army down the years while completely ignoring the appearance of the many foreign units which have played their part in the military history of the North American continent. At what stage did that army become American, in any event? Were the soldiers who fought in provincial volunteer units against the French in the 1750s any less American for being members of the forces of the British Crown? What nationality was Robert Rogers, born and raised in Massachusetts, the terror of the French and Indians in 1760 and the founder of a Tory corps to fight against the patriot colonists in the 1770s? There are many vague lines of demarcation which could be drawn, many pedantic definitions which would exclude this or that regiment. Unashamedly anxious to include the colourful figures of Englishman, Frenchman, Dutchman, German, Swiss, Spaniard, Mexican and Canadian as well as that of the American of three centuries, we have cast the net wide and risked the irritation of the purist.

Despite the generous facilities for colour illustrations provided by the publishers, a story as colourful, as turbulent, and, at times, as frankly confusing as that of the development of military power in America is vastly too rich to be captured in real depth in any one book. We have agonised over the selection of the colour plates, and believe that we have arrived at a reasonably well balanced result – but we are all too well aware of the omissions. Among the areas which we acknowledge to be sadly, but unavoidably weak are the uniforms of Canadian and Spanish formations; and with the exception of a single figure who may be said to be wearing 'military dress' of a sort, we have had to ignore the race who have the greatest claim of all – the American Indians. To have included a mere handful of figures illustrating isolated aspects of their story would, we feel, have been worse than excluding them entirely.

The most concise description of the material which we offer the reader of this book would be that it is a brief survey of the appearance of fighting men in North America from the mid-17th Century to the present day, with a heavy emphasis on the uniforms of the armed forces of the Federal government once truly national forces had emerged, but including some illustrations and descriptions of the enemies and allies of those forces on American soil. Because real history is always written, we believe, by the common soldier rather than the general, we have resolved any conflicting claims by concentrating on the ordinary infantryman, the trooper and the junior company officer of the combat branches rather than on the senior officer and the specialist non-combatant – though examples of both these categories will be found in this book.

Our approach is basically chronological. Each chapter begins with a necessarily brief survey of military activity, or the nature of the soldier, in the period in question. The second half of each chapter consists of detailed commentaries on the colour plates relevant to that chapter. We have not sought to describe the progress of wars and campaigns in any great detail, because this is, after all, a book on military dress rather than on military operations; but we have tried to block in the background, believing that the reader will find the plates more rewarding if supported by some idea of the character and experiences of the soldiers illustrated. We naturally hope that some of the figures will be entirely new to the reader, and that this book will open up for him fascinating new areas of interest. To the European the phrase *US Army* immediately conjours up a few well-known associations: blue-shirted cavalry charging into action at Apache Pass and the Powder River, the Little Bighorn and Adobe Walls; ragged grey riflemen boiling up the ridges of Gettysburg with low-thrust bayonets, yelling like maniacs; vast tides of olive-drab GI Joes hacking across France and Germany. But American military history is far broader and richer than these few hackneyed moments, and we hope that at least some readers will share our enthusiasm for the more obscure but equally dramatic chapters of the story by the time they reach the last page.

We could not have attempted the compilation of this book without drawing on the generosity of many friends and the published researches of dozens of other writers. Those who have contributed most are listed below, but to all of them we extend our sincere gratitude.

First on any list of acknowledged sources must be the Company of Military Historians, that excellent and dedicated American society whose series of superb plates must be the major source of any compilation in this field. We make no attempt to disguise the debt which this book owes to their published researches, and would like to record our respect for their tremendous achievements. We have also received much kind advice and active help from Phil and Rebecca Katcher and Bob Crisman of the 1st Pennsylvania Loyalists, and from David Scheinmann; together with Mike Robson, Marcus Hinton, Max Sarche, Joe Rosa, Mrs. Anna S. K. Brown and Fred Wilkinson, they have been of the greatest assistance in the assembly of illustrations. Our thanks also to Jim Jocelyn, Bob Marrion, David Damper and Jack Woodhouse, to Henry Davis Jr of the Patton Museum of Cavalry and Armor at Fort Knox, to the staffs of the Imperial War Museum and Radio Times Hulton Picture Library, to the United States National Archives (General Services Administration), and to the Prints Room of the New York Public Library.

May 1972   *MCW, GAE*

1 Colonial Arena

Military activity in the areas of eastern America settled by European immigrants in the 17th and 18th Centuries was governed from the outset by three main factors: geographical isolation, varying political climates in Europe, and the independent nature of the colonists themselves.

By 1646 some 27,000 colonists from Britain had arrived in the areas then known as New England, Maryland and Virginia, and were engaged in a struggle to establish communities along the edge of a vast and menacing wilderness. Among these coastal settlements were others founded during the same period by colonists from Holland and Sweden; and inland, following the line of the St Lawrence River and the Great Lakes, was the main belt of potentially hostile French settlements. Between the two, and all around the isolated settlements of both nationalities, were the Indians – sometimes placid or actively friendly, sometimes savagely hostile.

During the century between roughly 1650 and 1760 the shape of these settled areas would gradually develop. The English colonies would become more diverse and would develop local identities, culminating in the emergence of the Thirteen Colonies of the revolutionary period. They would expand westward and southward into the hinterland until, one by one, they came up against an increasingly strong French presence – either the physical presence of French forts and trading posts, or the territories of Indians who had come under French influence. The French would extend their posts and settlements in a southwesterly direction from the St Lawrence and the Great Lakes, and in a north-easterly direction up the great Ohio Valley from their other footholds in Louisiana. The threat of a continuous belt of French-dominated territory from the Gulf of Mexico to the St Lawrence

and the Atlantic slowly emerged. The danger that the English colonies would be penned forever behind the Appalachian Mountains, their frontiers exposed to the activities of Indians under French direction, led to several open wars between French and English settlers and their client Indians; eventually, with the coming of the Seven Years War in Europe, the wars in America would be escalated by the arrival of large numbers of French and British regular troops, and the future of the English colonies would be assured on the Heights of Abraham. While the sporadic confrontations of French and English continued, the smaller colonies of Dutch and Swedish stock would slowly disappear; their rights would be taken from them in a series of petty skirmishes, usually sparked off by naked ambition in the trading field, and the vastly greater size and birthrate of the English colonies would submerge them.

An analogy which may help to convey the nature of the early conflicts in North America would be a situation in which several powerful nations established colonies on, say, Mars.

The parent nations are involved in an almost perpetual power struggle on Earth, with wars and treaties following one another at short intervals; and they expect their colonies on Mars to reflect the volatile situation on Earth by taking the field against one another. The difficulties of communication between Earth and Mars lead to confusion and needless tragedies. Even in times of ostensible peace on Earth the Mars colonies are encouraged to deliver pin-prick raids on one another; if they succeed they can be pursued, if they fail they can be disowned by the parent government. Both sides have their own allies, more or less unpredictable, among the native Martian population, which is scattered across an inhospitable wilderness in small savage clans. The colonists stir up their Martian allies to attack enemy colonies, or the favoured clans of the enemy. The situation is further complicated by occasional murderous rampages by Martian clans acting on their own initiative. But the governing factor is always the isolation of the colonists from Earth; all parties concerned must exist, and mount operations, in a

English military wheelock pistol of the mid-17th Century, typical of the type of personal weapon which might have been carried by the early colonists. *Bennet Collection*

The powder horn was an almost universal piece of equipment; some examples were finely carved and stained, some carried maps, others had compasses mounted on the plug. This is the large type, as used by master-gunners. *Gyngell Collection*

Soldier of one of the New England Independent Companies of colonial militia, in the dress of the 1670s. These formations bore the brunt of such campaigns as King Philip's War (1675-76) and Queen Anne's War, at the turn of the century. Their exposure to the Indian, and later the French threat, made the New England colonies less inept, militarily, than the more southerly settlements. This soldier wears a heavy 'buff coat', with the sleeves tied in place with 'points'. He supplements his dog-lock musket with a hatchet for close fighting, carried slung in an old sword baldric. *Artist's Collection*

totally hostile environment and against a background of the common struggle simply to survive local conditions. They can spare only a fraction of their time and manpower for military activity, or they will perish together. Only sporadically supplied from Earth, they must improvise every necessity from local materials, with great labour. Materials from Earth can only be transported in small amounts, at great cost and after unpredictable delays. The effort required to maintain any force under arms is, relatively, enormously greater than on Earth; clashes which would be negligible patrol actions on Earth assume, on Mars, the importance of great battles. The hazards of simply moving from one colony to another are enormous, and many expeditions vanish without trace, victims of the environment rather than the enemy.

Regular troops from Britain and France only rarely ventured to America in the 17th and early 18th Centuries, and their despatch was usually motivated by reports of internal unrest within the colonies – to which the home governments were always sensitive – rather than by external threats. In times of war the settlements depended for their survival on their militia. The male inhabitants of military age were required to present themselves, properly outfitted and armed, for periodic training, and to answer the call of the colonial governor in times of crisis. The call-up would normally be on a strictly local basis and for a strictly limited period. The frequency and efficiency of training musters tended to be considerable in exposed frontier communities, but naturally became less impressive as the frontiers advanced and the immediate threat receded westwards. There was little tradition of co-operation between towns within the same colony, let alone between different colonies; as the money to support armed

expeditions had to be provided by the local assemblies there was a tendency to regard any alleged emergency from a narrow local standpoint. The command of the local militia would generally be in the hands of locally prominent families, and was decided by popular vote rather than by any consideration of military skill. While the militia organisation was a continuous infrastructure, the occasional requirement to mount expeditions of an offensive nature beyond the boundaries of the community was usually met by a call for volunteers. These men would also assemble for a strictly defined period and purpose, and were often prone to changes of heart at awkward moments. The motives which prompted local figures to put themselves forward for commissions to command these parties did not always bear too close scrutiny. (This distinction between militia and volunteers has proved impossible to maintain throughout the text of this book; the two terms will hereafter be used loosely, to describe local civilian levies assembled for limited periods and commanded by leaders of widely differing experience and ability.)

By the mid-18th Century the mutual suspicion which frequently crippled any attempt to mount co ordinated defensive or offensive operations was further aggravated by the stirring of nationalist ambitions within the colonies. The King's Governor of any colony found that he had to contend with the distrust of the local assemblies as well as the rapacity of the Indians and the ambitions of the French. The governor, a royal appointee sent out from England or selected from the reliable loyalist aristocracy of the colony, would call for troops to be raised to meet some emergency, perhaps – though by no means always – acting in concert with other governors. The money to support those levies had to be voted by the colonial assembly, and months might pass while the governor's motives were shrilly debated and examined, with an almost hysterical cynicism, for some ulterior plot – usually an imagined scheme to exert armed pressure on the assembly and the democratic rights of the local institutions. By the time the raising of troops was grudgingly permitted – often on a smaller scale than requested and hedged about with petty qualifications as to command responsibility and mission – it would be too late. The weeds would already be green among the ashes of the isolated settlements butchered and burned by Indians while the assembly wrangled; the flag of the Bourbons would already be flying over some new chain of blockhouses along the rivers and lakes, ensuring that the eventual ejection of the French would be that much harder and costlier.

These problems did not hamper New France, which was administered as a fief of a feudal monarchy. The French colonies were handicapped and eventually lost through a shortage of sufficient settlers to make France's vast territorial claims a reality; a shortsighted policy of religious intolerance limited immigration to Catholics, thus denying the province the enormous and able infusion of manpower which would have arrived in the thinly-held settlements if Huguenots had been permitted to enter. Despite this weakness in manpower the energy and success of the French authorities were impressive. From the earliest days of colonisation the French had handled their relations with the Indians with more subtlety and skill than the English, and thus were able to manipulate the tribes in such a way as to make up for their weakness in European manpower. Raiding parties were almost invariably composed mainly of Indians, with a few French soldiers or wood-crafty colonists in a supervisory capacity. This reliance on the

Typical British infantry private's coat of the 1750s. Colonial units probably wore coats of similar cut but without the decorations. This garment, which was usually worn with the skirts hooked for ease of marching and neatness, was made of a coarse brick-red cloth lined and faced with the regiment's colour. It was bound and decorated with the regimental lace, a white tape with distinctive coloured patterns and lines superimposed. The buttons were pewter. Contemporary sources state that coats were worn inside out by troops on sea journeys and fatigues, and men undergoing punishment. *Artist's Collection*

Indians to do most of the actual fighting had a ghastly consequence; the barbarous standards of Indian warfare came to be widely accepted as normal by Europeans. White men, both French and British, set the red man on their white enemies without scruple, and the horrible fate of white settlers at Indian hands was ignored or even welcomed. The offering of scalp bounty was a purely European innovation.

The French manipulated their Indians partly by means of religion. Jesuit missionaries doubled as intelligence officers and guerilla leaders, and fed the tribes with carefully edited versions of the Christian faith. Bearing in mind the universal zeal of new converts to any idea, the results of teaching the savages that Christ was a Frenchman crucified by Englishmen can be readily imagined – especially when the lesson was accompanied by liberal distribution of the other two pillars of Franco-Indian relations, brandy and muskets. The men who ran rotgut whisky and rifles to the Plains tribes in the mid-19th Century were merely the inheritors of an old-established business.

The actual conduct of all fighting in those early days followed only two patterns, the defensive and the offensive. Close-order pitched battles were out of the question for obvious reasons. The wooded hills ruled out European-style manoeuvres, there were never enough men to assemble massed battalions, and the independent spirit of the colonists – who were, after all, refugees from European regimentation and authority – rebelled against the discipline required for this sort of fighting. The scarcity of game made it impossible to maintain large groups of men in the field for any length of time, even if they would have consented; in the forest starvation was always a threat, and more than one armed party were reduced to grubbing for roots and berries as they struggled to regain their stockades. In times of crisis the inhabitants of a settlement, with their beasts and what goods they could carry, would take refuge behind stout log walls and pallisades and try to beat off the attackers with musket, blunderbuss and hatchet. If the numbers involved were not too uneven they usually had a good chance of survival. The Indians fought in loosely disciplined war-parties, and often lost interest and went in search of easier pickings if the initial defence was determined and effective. In the numerous cases where the Indians fell upon some small settlement without warning, of course, the story was very different. In the forests the Indians were supreme; their whole culture, based upon hunting, fitted them for a war of silent stalking and ambush. Many a successful defence of a stockade was followed by tragedy when overconfident settlers tried to follow the

Reproduction—typical frontier militiaman of the mid-18th Century. The checked shirt (popular even at this early date), the knee breeches and the simple linen smock are all copied from everyday civilian dress of the period, as are the slouch hat and buckled shoes. Leather equipment and brass-hilted hanger are typical military items, issued by the local armoury in time of emergency, as were military muskets. *Katcher*

Indians into the forest in search of vengeance.

Gradually the settlers adapted to the Indian's skills. The solitary trappers and hunters who lived a harsh and uncertain life along the fringes of the colonies picked up the essential disciplines of forest living and forest fighting, and formed a nucleus in times of trouble, no less crafty and no less ruthless than the tribesmen themselves. They also enjoyed the advantages of far superior weapons and far greater practice in their use. The Indians soon acquired firearms, but were always short of ammunition, and were seriously handicapped by the lack of resident craftsmen to repair or replace their guns. The fringed buckskin hunting shirt and the long, deadly accurate flintlock rifle became the trademarks of the tough, self-sufficient trappers, who provided a hard core of guides and raiders in time of war. Often they lived with the Indians, took Indian wives, and only returned to the settlements once or twice a year to sell their pelts and stock up with necessities. These men were to be found along the frontiers of both the French and the English colonies, and it was from their ranks that the French 'Woods-Runners' and the British 'Rangers' were recruited during the great French-Indian Wars of the mid-18th Century.

While the frontiersmen could scout and raid and burn and butcher, they could not seize, fortify and hold – and in the final analysis it was to be the holding of forts which would decide who ruled the waterways of Canada and the valleys of America. In the early stages of the French-Indian Wars expeditions of colonial volunteers were mounted to seize French forts or build British ones; generally these expeditions turned out to be fiascoes owing to the more professional approach of the French adversary. When British regulars appeared on the scene in the 1750s the picture changed, and throughout a decade of see-saw warfare the grip of the English-speaking colonies on French life-lines tightened, until the final victory. The popular picture of the English redcoats blundering through the forests in rigid, cumbersome formations, falling like flies to the arrows and musket-balls of the wily Indians, is drawn from one or two isolated disasters and is not really a mature judgement. The appalling rout of Braddock's expedition against Fort Duquesne in July 1755 is often cited as an example of British military rigidity reaping its just rewards. Perhaps – but what of Lord Howe, who laboured single-mindedly to turn his redcoats into forest fighters, and succeeded? What of the measured volleys of Wolfe's regiments on the Heights of Abraham, blasting France out of North America by just the same methods employed by their grandfathers at Blenheim and Ramillies fifty years before? The new continent was finally won by an intelligent combination of locally trained rangers and riflemen, friendly Indians, and regulars, each committed to battle under the conditions which suited them best.

Areas of national settlement in about 1740; at this time Spain still held coastal strips in eastern and western Florida and along the Gulf coast.

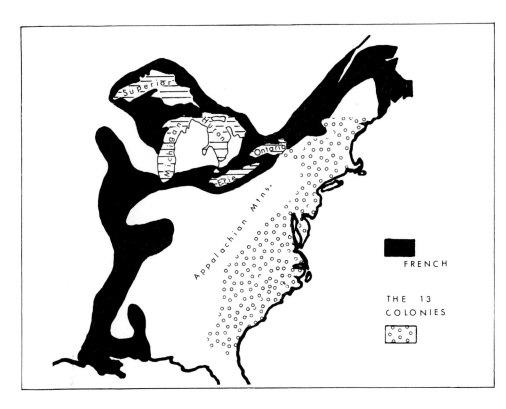

FRENCH

THE 13 COLONIES

Development of the hunting shirt. The three on the *left* are typical linen or homespun 18th Century shirts, derived from the simple smock of the farmer and labourer of the day. They were dyed a variety of shades or worn in the natural unbleached state, sometimes with coloured fringes; made by the womenfolk, they displayed a wide range of decoration including stitched hearts and elaborate pleats. General Washington's contractors mass-produced them during the War of Independence—he considered the hunting shirt a neat, simple and practical substitute for conventional uniform. *Upper right* is a typical military pattern of the early 19th Century; in green linen with yellow fringes, and cut with the high collar and tight sleeves of the day, this was the official summer campaign dress of the regular US Regiment of Riflemen. *Low right* is an example of an even later style—the type of smock worn well into the Civil War by many of the volunteer companies of the 1860s. *Artist's collection*

PLATES 1,2,3

1. Lieutenant, Netherlands Corps of Marines, New York, 1673

New Amsterdam changed hands several times in the late 17th Century; captured by English colonists in 1664 and renamed New York, it was recaptured in the summer of 1673 by 600 Dutch Marines led by Captain Anthony Colve. The city and surrounding areas were occupied until a treaty of February 1674 led to their being handed back to the English. The Netherlands Corps of Marines was established in 1665 as a distinct arm of the States General, on the advice of de Ruyter and de Witt. Initially the Marines are believed to have worn the same clothing as other Dutch troops of the day, with the omission of the steel cuirass then generally worn. By 1672, however, a special uniform appears to have evolved, and it is illustrated here.

A brown beaver hat without decorations, a blue collarless coat with yellow cuffs and pewter buttons, and knee-breeches were worn by all ranks. Ordinary soldiers wore the linen shirt collar outside the coat, in place of the officers' neck-cloth illustrated here. The colour of the breeches seems to have varied – brown, grey and red were all used. The stockings were either grey or blue wool. High soft leather boots seem to have been optional wear for officers. The orange sash distinguished officers and sergeants, and the gorget, bearing a crossed anchor motif, identified the rank of officers by the colour of its velvet backing piece – blue for captains, black for lieutenants, and white for ensigns. Sergeants and corporals wore white lace distinctions on the right shoulder, and corporals carried a small cane, often hooked to a coat button for convenience.

The sword, its scabbard suspended in a broad leather baldric, was worn by all ranks. Enlisted men were armed with a flintlock or snaphaunce musket and a plug bayonet; officers carried the half-pike or espontoon, but a published source states that these were not much in evidence on shipboard or landing parties, and a flintlock or snaphaunce pistol would probably have been thrust into the sash.

2. Fusilier, Regiment de Carignan-Sallières, New France, 1665-68

The Regiment of *Carignan-Sallières*, named after its first and its present colonels, was shipped from La Rochelle to Quebec in the spring of 1665, arriving in June. Its task was to assist the Canadian militia and their Algonquin

Indian allies in a war against the Iroquois, who were friendly to the British colonists. This they did, with some success but not without loss. This regiment was thus the first major regular unit of any European army to be posted to North America.

Much has been published about the uniform of this regiment, and several illustrations have appeared, not all of them soundly based on known fact. We have attempted to limit our illustration to features which can be confirmed from 17th Century material. The French infantry of the day wore no regulation uniform, and colonels were enjoined merely to see that their men were 'well clothed and well shod'. It is believed that this unit were equipped with dark brown frieze coats with deep, button-back cuffs, and with breeches of the same colour. The wide-brimmed black felt hat, occasionally trimmed with coloured tape, was common wear among French troops of the day. Buttons were covered with cloth of the same colour as the coat. During their Canadian service the soldiers would certainly have acquired locally made items such as scarves and mittens of coarse wool, and the use of Indian-style cloth leggings, thonged in place, is believed to have dated from the earliest days of colonisation.

A coarse linen bag tied with cords so that it could be slung around the shoulders is typical of the period; haversacks suspended from straps did not come into general use until the 18th Century. Waistbelts were not generally issued among French troops of this period.

The armament of French infantry of the mid-17th Century was mixed, each company containing a proportion of pikemen, musketeers with matchlock weapons, and non-commissioned officers with swords and pistols. The use of the flintlock *fusil* and the plug bayonet was a matter of controversy at this time; only a small proportion of the musketeers were armed in this way. We have illustrated a *fusilier,* as various sources maintain that the *Carignan-Sallières* were the first regiment to be equipped completely with this weapon; but the date of this step cannot be confirmed, nor the exact equipment of the unit on its posting to the New World. Musketeers were issued with the broad crossbelt bearing eight or twelve wooden or horn containers for measured powder charges – the 'Twelve Apostles' – and an attached leather bag for bullets. The fusilier would carry two powder flasks, one for loading and another for the finer-grain priming powder, in addition to his bullet-bag. In the field,

hatchets often replaced the issue swords.

The pale blue and yellow distinctions attributed to the uniform of the regiment by various sources cannot be confirmed for this period, and, if correct, may well refer to a later date after two companies had returned to France to form the nucleus of a new regiment. The only further point about this uniform which can be made with confidence is that as time wore on such items of dress as were brought from France would have been replaced increasingly by locally obtained materials in various coarse and simply-dyed weaves, and by fur and hide garments.

3. Musketeer, Jeffrey's Regiment, 1677

Jeffrey's Regiment had a short and relatively uneventful career, but is assured of a place in history as the first British regular regiment to serve in America. It was raised hastily from drafts of the Foot Guards, the Holland Regiment and the Maritime or Admiral's Regiment in 1676, and shipped to Virginia under the command of one Colonel Herbert Jeffrey. News had reached London that Governor Berkeley of that colony was beset by rebels led by one Nathaniel Bacon, and Herbert Jeffrey was ordered to restore the King's peace, take over from Berkeley as Lieutenant Governor of Virginia, and ship the ex-Governor home. When the regiment arrived in January 1677 they found the rebellion already crushed, and Governor Berkeley taking his revenge on any colonists he suspected of shaky loyalty by the well-tried method of mass hangings. Berkeley declined to comply with the Colonel's instructions, and had enough local supporters under arms to defy the scratch regiment from England. Jeffrey 'maintained a low profile' until he received orders to return home a year later. Some of his men were allowed to remain in Virginia as planters.

The regiment was uniformed in the conventional style of the day, while the various companies retained some features of the uniforms of their original units. The musketeer illustrated – the British infantry was still a mixed force of pikes and muskets – retains the red leather bandolier and blue hat ribbon of his service with the First Foot Guards. The red coat with blue lining and the blue breeches are thought to have been issued to all companies of the regiment. Apart from the matchlock musket the soldier is armed with a sword slung in a baldric of buff leather. The bandolier supports the 'Twelve Apostles', a bullet bag and a spare length of match.

4. Private, Gooch's Regiment, 1741

At this period the British military establishment was of limited size and closely tailored to the nation's domestic needs. Any expedition abroad required the raising of extra regiments, an expensive proposition always hotly resisted by certain factions in the House of Commons, then as now. In addition to the expense, there was the difficulty of recruiting; unsophisticated as were the classes from which men were recruited in the 18th Century, most of them were bright enough to ask where they would be sent, and even at this early date the West Indies had acquired an evil reputation as a disease-ridden Hell. So when the War of Jenkins' Ear (the colonial war between Britain and Spain, 1739-43) broke out, the means by which operations in the Americas were to be mounted came under consideration.

Only three regiments were available in the New World, in addition to a number of independent local defence companies. Dalzell's Regiment was in the West Indies, Phillips' Regiment was at Annapolis, and Oglethorpe's Regiment was in Georgia; the latter unit was to see some brisk and successful fighting against Spanish troops along the Florida marches. When war broke out Alexander Spotswood, Governor of Virginia, was authorised to raise a regiment of foot from local volunteers, to be equipped by Britain, which would also provide a certain number of experienced veterans to assist the officers. All those colonies not committed to the struggle on the Florida frontier were expected to raise and support companies for the regiment, which was later committed to an extremely ill-managed and unsuccessful attempt to capture Cartagena. When this assault failed, largely due to lack of co-operation between the military and naval commanders, the unit was sent to Santiago de Cuba, and, still without a victory to its name, to Portobello. Its very heavy casualties were largely due to disease and the neglect of the commanders of the expedition. In the meantime Spotswood had died, and the regiment was known variously as 'Gooch's' and 'The American Regiment'. It was disbanded in 1742.

The private illustrated wears the regulation uniform of the British infantry of the day, although once committed to action in the Indies the men would probably have discarded the coat and gaiters. The red coat, waistcoat and breeches were common to most units, and regimental distinctions appear in the form of coloured cuffs and coat facings – in the case of this unit, light green. The coat is lined with coarse linen for tropical service, visible on the turn-backs. There is no lace – that is, decorative edging around the borders of coat facings and cuffs and the waistcoat – and this unit thus displays a rather utility appearance. The black tricorn hat, decorated with white tape and a black cockade, was common to most contemporary regiments. Equipment comprises buff leather belts with brass buckles, the waistbelt supporting a frog for the socket bayonet and the brass-hilted sword – the latter was often discarded – and the crossbelt carrying the black leather cartridge box. The flintlock musket, an early version of the type universally known as 'Brown Bess', has brass furniture. In the absence of a canteen this soldier is following a common practice of the 18th Century, and using a bound and shaped gourd slung on a cord.

5. Sergeant, Swiss Regiment Karrer, 1745
The fortress of Louisbourg, a major French defensive work on Cape Breton Island, guarded the strategically vital approaches to the St Lawrence. A stone-built fort and batteries designed on conventional European lines was a rarity in the Americas, where timber and earth were the usual materials for field works. Despite its strong position and excellent design the fortress was twice captured, once by New England volunteers supported by the firepower of the Royal Navy, and once by British regulars. The causes of the fall of the fortress are believed to have been inadequate armament, supplies, garrisons, and supporting operations.

The capture of Louisbourg by Pepperell's inexperienced but spirited provincial troops in 1745 was the first indication that volunteers could achieve results of which regulars would be proud, if they were properly led, properly supported, and inspired by genuine enthusiasm. It was a severe shock to French complacency, and a fitting response to France's apathetic treatment of her splendid fortress. The French attitude appeared to be that its very excellence would deter any attacker; consequently the garrison was allowed to run to seed through a failure to provide regular pay and decent living conditions, many of the gun positions were never equipped with cannon, and inadequate stores were layed in. The regular garrison in 1745, which was intended to be reinforced by militia in times of emergency, totalled less than 600 men. This mixed force comprised eight companies of colonial marines (see **8,** Plate 2), two companies of mercenaries from the Swiss *Karrer*

Regiment, and an artillery detachment.

This sergeant, carrying on the age-old tradition of Swiss mercenary soldiering, wears the red coat often found among French mercenary troops of the period. This regiment was specifically raised for colonial service in 1721, and detachments served in various posts throughout New France. The uniform of all ranks was a red coat with blue cuffs, blue waistcoat and breeches, and white gaiters; the black tricorn hat was decorated with a black ribbon cockade and white tape. The sergeant's rank is indicated by the silver braiding around the top of the coat cuffs, and he is armed with a halberd rather than the 1717 model French musket carried by the rank and file. All ranks wore the short, straight, brass-hilted sword.

It is recorded that although the Swiss companies were on the verge of mutiny against their conditions in 1745, they fought bravely during the British attack. After the surrender of Louisbourg they were repatriated to France, where they faced a searching investigation into their earlier mutinous behaviour; several were hanged.

6. Private, Battalion Company, British 44th Regiment of Foot, 1755
There is no space in this book for a detailed account of Braddock's Massacre of 1755; the present writer can do no better than recommend the hideously vivid description in Parkman's *Montcalm and Wolfe*. Briefly, Major-General Edward Braddock arrived in America in February 1755 to lead the British 44th and 48th Regiments of Foot and various provincial volunteer units on an expedition against the French in the Ohio Valley. The regiments were assembled and brought up to strength at Alexandria, Virginia, and in June set off to do what the local militiamen had failed to do – drive the French from Ft Duquesne on the Forks of the Ohio. The column, hampered by its wagons in the wooded country, became dangerously spread out. On July 9th, in close terrain, it was ambushed by some 650 Indians, 150 French-Canadians, and French regulars in company strength. Braddock tried to fight the concealed enemy with the close-order manoeuvres and massed fire which he understood from more than forty years' service in Europe; the result was a rout. Braddock paid with his life, as did a large proportion of his regulars; their formations broken, their officers dead, without clear orders and under a withering fire from the whooping tribesmen in the dark eaves of the forest, the

survivors broke and fled. A ghastly scene followed as the Indians stripped, tortured and scalped the fallen, but the delay enabled the survivors to escape.

The gear carried by this private of a battalion company of the 44th (each regiment contained one company of grenadiers, the remaining companies being termed 'battalion') shows certain innovations which acquit Braddock of the charge of total lack of imagination often levelled at him. He made a genuine effort to fit his men for forest service, ordering them to leave their waistbelts and swords, crossbelts and bulky equipment with the wagons. It must be assumed that the cartridge boxes were worn on a narrow waist strap, in the manner of the grenadiers in the well-known paintings by David Morier. The bayonet would presumably have been thrust into this strap when not required. The white, buttoned gaiters of the normal dress order were replaced, at Braddock's order, by the harder wearing brown canvas marching gaiters. The waistcoat and breeches were of a light-weight material for the spring campaign. Other surviving orders which show Braddock in a better light are his insistence that the men be given pads to wear under their hats to protect them from sunstroke, and a warning of severe punishment for any man found encumbering his musket on the march by attaching tent poles to it for easy carrying. A tin water flask and a knapsack were worn on straps over the right shoulder.

The basic red uniform of the British infantry is distinguished here by the yellow facings and decorative lace of the 44th – the latter white with yellow, blue and black threads woven into it in a complex pattern. Sergeants wore red waist sashes and swords, but carried muskets instead of halberds; officers were ordered to replace their espontoons with fusils, or short flintlock muskets, as normally issued to artillerymen.

7. Corporal of Grenadiers, French Infantry Regiment Béarn, 1755-60
The *Béarn* Regiment was one of several French regular units which will always be renowned for their service in Canada during the French-Indian War; other units involved were the *La Reine, Languedoc, Guyenne, Royal Roussillon, Berry* and *La Sarre* Regiments. The *Béarn* was formed from a battalion of the *Picardie* regiment in 1684, and by the time it was shipped to New France in 1755 it had seen service in the Palatinate, Flanders, Italy,

Germany and Corsica The regiment fought at Niagara and Oswego in 1756 and in the capture of Fort William Henry (immortalised in Cooper's *The Last of the Mohicans*) in 1757. It fought on the right flank, under the Chevalier de Lévis, in the defence of Fort Carillon (Ticonderoga) in 1758. After the loss of Canada it returned to France, and was disbanded in 1762.

The French infantry uniform of the day was a grey-white coat and breeches and a black tricorn hat; regiments were identified by the colour of coat collar and cuffs and the colour of the long, sleeved waistcoat worn under the coat. The distinctions of the *Béarn* were red collars, cuffs, and waistcoat; the cut of the pockets and placing of the buttons were also peculiar to each regiment. Other examples are the *Languedoc's* blue collar, cuffs and waistcoats, and the *La Sarre's* blue collar and cuffs and red waistcoat. Identification could be complicated by the fact that troops frequently removed their coats and fought in waistcoats in summer.

'False gold' lace and a black cockade were the usual hat decorations, though the colour of the former varied with the regiment. Sergeants wore a band of gold lace around the top of the cuff; this man's three yellow braid cuff-loops are his corporal's insignia. Normal field equipment comprised wide buff straps with brass furniture; a crossbelt supported the cartridge box, a waistbelt the double frog on the left hip for sword and bayonet. Grenadiers wore a large, ornate pouch, but this merely commemorated their former function, and was used for cartridges in the normal way. They also wore a broad-bladed sabre in place of the straight *épee* of fusiliers, and were allowed moustaches. Swords were often discarded, and hatchets carried in their place or in addition. The simple *de la Parterie* pack is a linen bag with a carrying strap passed under the flap, which is then tied with cord. Officers wore very similar uniforms, distinguished by gorgets and lace-decorated waistcoats; in the field velvet breeches and buckled leather leggings were popular. On campaign sergeants and officers often replaced their halberds and espontoons with fusils.

8. Private, Compagnies Franches de la Marine, 1755-60

Troops raised for service in the colonies were traditionally under the aegis of the French naval, rather than the military authorities, and until almost the present day colonial infantry were known as 'marines' despite their conventional infantry rôle. The *Compagnies Franches de la Marine,* or 'colony troops', were raised in 1690, and into the new organisation were absorbed those Marine companies which had been sent from France in various detachments since 1683. Thereafter men were sometimes recruited from the local male population; officers, originally sent from France, were increasingly commissioned from among the French-Canadian aristocracy. By 1757 there were forty companies of these troops on the establishment; they usually operated as independent commands, and each company had a strength of about sixty-five men. In the latter stages of the French-Indian War Montcalm assembled several companies into a Marine Battalion, and used it on the battlefield. The normal duties of the colony troops, however, were garrisoning isolated forts and settlements along the French lines of communication through the vast wilderness of Canada, and operating as raiders along with the 'Woods-Runners' and Indians. The recruiting standards for these companies were lower than those of the regulars.

The full dress of the colony troops comprised the familiar grey-white coat with a low stand-up collar and deep cuffs of the same colour, a blue waistcoat and blue breeches. White leggings or blue woollen stockings were worn, and the usual leather equipment and weapons were issued. The black tricorn hat was trimmed with 'false gold' and a black cockade. This soldier is illustrated in working dress. He has discarded his white coat and works in his long-sleeved waistcoat; for comfort and convenience on the logging detail, his tricorn hat has been abandoned in favour of a soft fatigue cap of blue cloth, decorated with yellow tape and a fleur-de-lys. The gaiters were very frequently replaced by the simpler and more practical *mitasses* or Indian-style leggings; these were made of coarse trade-cloth or of buckskin, and a variety of decorative fringes, beaded thongs or Indian quill-work would probably have been in evidence at any fort. Isolated as they were, the colony troops may be presumed to have improvised quite widely in their clothing and equipment. Certainly swords and stiff shoes would have been replaced by tomahawks and moccasins for raiding parties and patrols in the forest.

9. Private, Rogers' Rangers, 1758

French garrisons and supply parties were increasingly harassed during the War by British-organised Ranger companies, who also provided much invaluable intelligence on enemy strengths and movements, and carried out daring surprise raids deep in enemy territory. The most famous of these 'commando' units were the companies raised and led by Robert Rogers of Massachusetts. The original company performed such valuable work in 1755 that it was gradually expanded into a Corps – 'His Majesty's Independent Companies of Rangers' – and Rogers later rose to the rank of colonel in the British Army. Apart from the combat companies, Rogers established a Cadet Company to train British and provincial officers in fieldcraft.

Initially there was no allowance for providing clothes or equipment, and each man wore what he enlisted in or 'liberated' along the trail. Various styles of hunting smocks and duffle or blanket coats, fur caps, and Indian items were all worn by these hand-picked scouts. In 1758 Rogers received an allowance to have uniforms made up especially for his unit, and the Ranger illustrated here wears the result. The Scots bonnet and jacket are of green frieze lined with serge, and the jacket has two rows of eight silver buttons down the front. Four more buttons are worn on the sleeve, and officers' jackets were distinguished by silver or white lace decoration around the buttonholes on the cuff. Buckskin breeches, Indian leggings and moccasins were highly practical dress for the type of fighting done by the Rangers; they were usually accompanied by parties of Stockbridge or Mohegan Indians in British pay. A simple pack is worn, containing the bare necessities of life in the forest – cornmeal and dried beef chips, spare moccasins, and so forth. A bullet pouch is worn on the belt, and a powder horn is slung around the body; sometimes a compass was fixed to the latter. A length of rope supports a wooden canteen. Knives and tomahawks were always carried, and the musket is fitted with a short knife-bayonet instead of the long regular infantry pattern, which would be unwieldy in the densely wooded country where the Rangers operated. This Ranger is examining an officer's gorget picked up on the trail; these marks of rank were worn by French and British alike, and were sometimes given to the chiefs who led their groups of Indian allies.

10. Major-General James Wolfe, Quebec, 1759

The young and much loved victor of the Heights of Abraham was sketched at the time by one of his aides, Captain Harvey Smythe, and this illustration is partly based on the details of that sketch. There was no regulation uniform for general officers at this period and, especially on campaign, they almost certainly dressed entirely according to personal taste – though in a generally 'military' manner. (It must be remembered that even half a century later the great Wellington fought most of his battles clad in a plain dark blue civilian frock coat.) Wolfe wears a red coat with red cuffs and lapel facing and two rows of gilt buttons. His waistcoat is also red and his breeches – in Smythe's sketch but not in a portrait later based upon it – are dark blue. His black cocked hat is decorated only by a black ribbon cockade, and he wears boots of the then-popular civilian style, soft black leather with tan turn-overs at the top. The black scarf around the arm, worn in mourning for his father, the fusil and the belt complete with bayonet frog are all from the Smythe sketch. The latter, worn in preference to a sword, may seem surprising for a general; but in an age when commanders were still quite frequently killed in action they represent a highly practical attitude. The heavy campaigning cloak has a hood, in this illustration worn folded back so that it resembles an upper cape collar.

11. Private, Battalion Company, 60th (Royal American) Regiment of Foot, 1757
The massacre of Braddock's regulars in 1755 caused something of a manpower crisis in America, and a few months later the British Parliament – not without misgivings – authorised the raising of a new type of unit from among the colonists. The 62nd Royal American Regiment (the number was changed to 60th in 1757) was to consist of four battalions recruited from the settlers in Pennsylvania and Maryland, and to a lesser extent from Massachusetts, New York and North Carolina; at a later date numbers of Englishmen joined the ranks of the regiment. The volunteers were thus to a large extent made up of men of Swiss and German stock, and the commanders of the first two battalions were Swiss professional soldiers – Henry Bouquet and Frederick Haldimand. The order which authorised the raising of the unit specified that up to fifty of the officers could be foreign Protestants, commissioned to serve only in the American colonies.

Surviving records give the impression of a unit which by the standards of the day was unusually spare, tough and efficient. The discipline and drill requirements were relaxed, and the whole emphasis of the training was upon

forest fighting. The soldier illustrated here displays some of the simplifications of uniform and equipment which distinguished this regiment. His red coat and waistcoat, faced with the blue of a Royal regiment, have no lace decorations. For campaign he wears hard-wearing leather breeches and brown canvas gaiters, in place of the cloth breeches and white gaiters worn with full dress. His coat is buttoned high, leaving two small 'wings' of the facing visible. His hair is cropped fairly short. His accoutrements consist of a musket and bayonet, a cartridge box, a haversack and a tin canteen.

The 60th, ancestors of the famous British King's Royal Rifle Corps, served with great distinction in all the major campaigns of the French-Indian War – at Ticonderoga, at Louisburg, at Quebec, and on expeditions to Martinique and Havana. The third and fourth battalions were disbanded in 1763, but the first and second remained in America until 1775.

12. Company officer, British Line Infantry on campaign, 1758
The uniform worn by this officer is a transitional style, typical of the period between the general acceptance that the formal European dress was useless for forest fighting, and the introduction of the official Light Infantry units. In 1758 Brigadier General Viscount Howe, a young British officer of great energy and foresight, issued orders concerning the outfitting of the men he was to lead on the expedition to Ticonderoga – an expedition on which he lost his life. Howe owed his popularity not only to his warm personality but also to his insistence on trying out any novelty for himself. He had accompanied Rogers' Rangers on an expedition, in order to study forest tactics, and was the first to comply with his own orders; orders not received with universal joy by fashionable officers.

He had his officers and men crop their hair to about an inch long. Their coat-tails were to be cut off, and all unnecessary decorations and equipment put aside. The men were to wear no swords, but were encouraged to acquire hatchets or tomahawks. In the field the heavy packs were to be left with the wagons and immediate necessities carried in a blanket-roll. Extra ammunition was issued, and the muskets were shortened and their bright metal fittings darkened. Ten rifled weapons, probably locally obtained German-style Jager rifles, were issued to the best shots in each infantry battalion; this officer has kept one for himself.

The cocked hats were cut down in a variety of styles, the most common being one in which a narrow circular brim was retained around the crown. The style shown here, with a single portion of the brim retained at the front and fixed upright, was to be the inspiration for the officially produced Light Infantry cap which appeared soon afterwards.

In the later stages of the war the various units were ordered to provide men for a unit of Light Infantry, picking those who were experienced at forest fighting, alert, energetic, and skilled shots. The original force was about 500 strong, including a detachment from the Royal Americans. They were carefully trained for bush fighting and dressed in a practical uniform evolved from the improvised style of Howe's men. The coat was discarded and sleeves sewn to the waistcoat; extra leather pockets were made, to hold flints and bullets, and leather leggings replaced the gaiters. The pack was replaced by a small haversack slung on a diagonal strap, and the tin canteen was covered with cloth. A buttoned case was made to hold the head of the hatchet, and ear-pieces were added to the small cap, which could be fastened under the chin in cold weather. Some of the light troops apparently went even further in their rejection of conventional uniform, and resembled rangers rather than regulars. The value of these skirmishers was such that in the aftermath of the French-Indian War several new regiments classified as 'Light Armed' were added to the British establishment; and, eventually, each infantry battalion was to have a Light Company on strength alongside the Grenadier Company and the Battalion Companies.

13. Private, Virginia Regiment, 1755-62
The first two companies of the Virginia Militia to be called up for service on the frontier were mustered and sent to build a fort at what is now Pittsburgh in 1754. The degenerating situation, heading inevitably towards a major war, prompted Governor Dinwiddie to increase the strength of his local forces to a regiment of six companies of volunteers later in the year; the first lieutenant-colonel of the regiment was a certain George Washington. After a brief period during which the regiment was broken up into independent companies it was incorporated once more in 1755 with a strength of sixteen companies, under the colonelcy of Washington. The unit provided several companies for Braddock's ill-fated expedition.

In the early days the men wore civilian clothing, but after the reorganisation of 1755, at Washington's urging, a uniform was authorised. While the first issue of military clothing to the regiment had been based on red coats of simple cut and cheap quality, the new uniform was, for reasons still uncertain, of dark blue. The coat is believed to have been 'bob-tailed' (shortened) in the fashion of that time, with scarlet facings and cuff decorations, a scarlet waistcoat, and blue breeches. The tricorn hat was of conventional appearance. Officers wore a similar uniform, with silver lace distinctions on the coat and waistcoat for full dress wear; in the field they were ordered to wear a common soldier's uniform. Field equipment and gaiters similar to those worn by British regulars of the day were doubtless provided; but in details of dress and equipment it is likely that there was a good deal of variation.

The regiment was finally disbanded in 1762 – but it was not to be the last time British soldiers saw George Washington at the head of a blue-coated regiment.

14. Private, Battalion Company, 42nd Regiment of Foot, 1758

One of the British units which distinguished itself in the heroic defeat of Abercromby's assault on Fort Carillon (Ticonderoga) in July 1758 was the 42nd Foot – the 'Black Watch', first Highland regiment in British service. Raised originally in 1739, the regiment arrived in America in June 1756 and underwent lengthy training in the type of fighting which they would be expected to carry out. With the 27th, 44th, 46th, 55th, and part of the 60th Regiments of Foot, and some 9,000 provincial volunteers, the Highlanders sailed down Lake George in July 1758 to attack Montcalm's highly strategic position at Fort Carillon on the narrow spit of land between Lakes George and Champlain. The Marquis de Montcalm himself commanded the garrison, brought up to a strength of some 2,500 regulars and the same number of colony troops and irregulars. The fort was protected by an extensive abbatis – an area of rough ground in front of the walls rendered almost impassable by ditches, hundreds of sharpened stakes, and a vast tangle of felled trees with their branches trimmed to points. This killing-ground, within musket range of the earthworks and commanded by batteries of artillery, was the scene of the Highlanders' epic charge. For nearly four hours the battle raged, as the British force struggled to hack their way through the abbatis

and take the breastworks of the fort. The obstacles effectively broke their ranks, and it quickly became a matter of each individual soldier struggling forward on his own initiative. The Highlanders left a deep impression on friend and foe alike; many, maddened with frustration, threw away their muskets and tried to cut their way through with their broadswords. Numbers of them actually mounted the breastwork, cutting footholds with their swords in the timber stockade, and were only thrown back with the greatest difficulty by the French defenders. At last, after the assault had suffered some 2,000 casualties including about 650 Highlanders, Abercromby withdrew his remaining companies; the 42nd covered the retreat and the recovery of the wounded. It is recorded that the order to retreat had to be given three times before the Highlanders heeded it.

The dress of the Highlanders in British service at this time was as illustrated here. A short scarlet jacket trimmed with regimental lace and with collars and cuffs in the regimental facing colour of buff was worn over a scarlet waistcoat. For formal occasions a voluminous belted plaid was worn, for campaign and service dress a kilt; the tartan, in the dark shades from which the regiment traditionally takes its name, had a red line in all kilts and in the plaids of the Grenadier Company only. Officers and men of the battalion companies wore a dark blue bonnet with a tuft of bearskin, and grenadiers a mitre cap with a heavy roach of the same fur. Broadswords were carried by all ranks, and in action officers and sergeants carried muskets like their men. At this period the sporran or goat-skin purse was of very simple design. For fatigues and other working details the Highlanders wore canvas breeches and leggings instead of their kilts.

Shortly after the Ticonderoga disaster the regiment received word that it had been rated a Royal unit – the 42nd (Royal Highland) Regiment of Foot – and the facing of the uniform was therefore changed from buff to blue. The regiment saw active service under Amherst in 1759, and in several Revolutionary War campaigns between 1776 and 1783.

15. Captain, 11th New Hampshire Regiment, 1774

The years following the surrender of Canada to British rule were not peaceful. The Cherokees rose in the southern colonies, isolating forts and settlements and taking many scalps. The great Pontiac made a name for

himself around Niagara and Detroit which is still part of American folklore. In this unquiet atmosphere many of the colonies kept their militia in good repair, and large numbers of volunteer units, briefly formed into Independent Companies and sometimes assembled into Provincial Regiments, saw active service. Together with the veterans of the French/Indian War this residue of ready-blooded soldiers was to stand the colonies in good stead in the coming revolution. Along the wilder frontiers of the colonies the long struggle with the Indians went on unchecked, and the end of French involvement meant little.

A typical Provincial unit was the 11th New Hampshire Regiment; the colony had a well-maintained militia, and a total of twelve regiments existed on paper. Such energy was encouraged by the London administration, who hoped both to shift some of the trouble and expense of defending the colonies on to Provincial rather than regular units, and to underpin the loyalty of the province. The rank and file drilled occasionally, and held themselves ready for emergency call-up; they would have worn no uniform. Officers, on the other hand, wore dress prescribed by the Governor, as Captain-General of Militia. This is basically British in character, and some five years behind current British Army fashion; from 1768 onwards the waistcoats and breeches of all British infantry units were buff or white. The company officer illustrated here wears the red coat lined, faced and cuffed in sky blue, with a sky blue waistcoat and breeches and white tape decorations.

PLATE 1

1

3

4

2

5

PLATE 2

6

7

8

9

10

PLATE 3

11

13

14

12

15

2 The Great Rebellion

This book is no place for a detailed discussion of the many political and social factors which tipped the thirteen colonies of North America into armed rebellion against the British throne in 1775. Suffice it to say that heavy-handed measures taken by the British military and political proconsuls following the 'Boston Tea Party' in December 1773 aggravated local resentments to such an extent that by September 1774 the First Continental Congress had assembled, and the representatives of the various colonial communities were taking practical steps to safeguard their liberty. Revolutionary governments in each colony moved to take over control of the local militia companies, replacing loyalist officers and taking custody of military stores. A third – the younger and more active third – of each town's militia were organised as 'Minutemen', ready to report for action at short notice.

In April 1775 Major General Thomas Gage, the commander of the British troops in America and a survivor of Braddock's Massacre, sent a force from Boston to Concord, Massachusetts, to seize or destroy a store of arms and ammunition. Alerted by Paul Revere and William Dawes, a small force of Minutemen barred the advance of the redcoats at Lexington. A nervous, but to this day unidentified hand squeezed off the 'shot that was heard round the world', and the frustrated regulars, without waiting for orders, sent a volley into the colonists, killing eight of them; the rest fled. The British force continued to Concord and carried out their mission; but for the whole return journey they suffered from continual sniping, as the colonists along their route seized their muskets and hunting rifles and closed in through the hedgerows, walls and thickets. A relief force had to be sent out to bring the column in, and the British suffered nearly 300 casualties. The flame of rebellion

Contemporary drawing of an American soldier, in fringed hunting shirt and some kind of Light Infantry-style cap. This sketch was drawn and published by Johann Martin Will of Augsburg in 1776, the source being a Bavarian officer who served in the British forces in America. *Anna S. K. Brown Military Collection*

caught, and soon armed colonists were assembling in every province. Boston itself came under seige, and rebels occupied the British posts at Ticonderoga and Crown Point and seized the cannon there.

In May 1775 Gage was reinforced by new regiments, bringing his strength up to about 6,500, and by three generals from England: Howe, Clinton and Burgoyne. The following month the rebels began entrenching on Breed's Hill, a position overlooking Boston from the north; intending to answer this provocation with a taste of what regular troops could do to raw farmers when they set their mind to it, Howe took about 2,200 men across the harbour to dislodge the rebels on June 17th.

The colonists held their fire until the redcoats had struggled up the slopes to within fifty yards of their improvised defences; when they finally opened up the effect was devastating, and the British lines broke and fell back. A second time the regulars formed up and charged up the hill, and a second time a withering fire thinned their ranks and sent them into retreat. The survivors rallied, and faced the ghastly slope again; and the third time, scrambling over the bodies of their comrades and the writhing wounded who covered the slippery grass, they carried the crest with the bayonet. Howe had his victory – at a cost of more than 1,000 casualties out of 2,200 engaged, against the rebels' 400 casualties. The lessons of Breed's (or Bunker) Hill were several. Farmers, inspired by a genuine cause, had stood up against the British redcoat and broken his ranks twice in succession. Some, it is true, had run, when they saw that inexorable line of bayonets coming out of the smoke a third time. Eye-witness reports speak of wounded men carried to the rear by as many as twenty eager volunteers. But this was understandable, and those who had not run

had achieved something like a miracle. Bunker Hill became a monument in the minds of the colonists, and morale soared. The redcoats, who had gathered their shocked and tattered ranks together and faced the hill that third decisive time, went stolidly back to their camps; they too had performed a small miracle, a miracle of steadiness and discipline and loyalty, but it was not the fashionable type of miracle in the climate of opinion which prevailed in the colonies.

Until the summer of 1775 only short-term New England volunteers were under arms, but in June the Second Continental Congress adopted the 'army' as its own and units from other colonies began to arrive. The first national army of American citizens consisted of the Massachusetts and Connecticut volunteers, some companies of riflemen from Pennsylvania, Maryland and Virginia, and a single artillery unit from Massachusetts; at their head Congress placed a Virginia gentleman with some experience of leading troops in action, named George Washington. Despite his service in the French-Indian War Washington was the first to acknowledge his lack of preparation for the size of operation which he was now going to have to control; but he was picked as much for his personal qualities and for the effect on southern public opinion as for his formal skills. These personal qualities would be tested to the full by the motley crowd which he now commanded. Disorganised, ill-disciplined and contentious, each local contingent had engaged for different lengths of time, carried different weapons, and pressed different opinions. Officers were elected by their men, and dismissed when the fancy took them. This high-spirited rabble was without training, supplies, proper camps or sanitary discipline, and without any feeling of commitment to a central rather than a local loyalty.

Centre
Reproduction—Continental private of 1776 on guard duty. The knitted stocking cap and blue checked shirt were both common items. The short brown civilian coat has 'mariner's cuffs'; the white linen overall trousers are of a style particularly approved by Washington. The ammunition for the French Charleville musket is carried both in the leather 'belly box' and in a tin canister slung on his right side; these latter were recommended at the time due to the leather shortage. The belt for the cartridge box also supports the bayonet scabbard on the left side, here obscured.

Left
Reproduction—the clothes and equipment of the Loyalist soldier of the War of Independence. At first as motley as their rebel enemies, and later dressed in green coats, the Provincial Corps had, by 1778, acquired brick red coats like their British regular comrades. The white smallclothes are worn with a black stock and black cloth half-gaiters. The coat is faced in dark green, with simple white tape decoration at the buttonholes; the pewter buttons bear the crowned *RP* cypher of the Royal Provincials. Belts are standard British issue buff leather, and the black cartridge box has a brass plate backed with red coat cloth. The black felt hat is bound with white and has a black cockade. The Long Land Model musket was carried mainly by Provincials and grenadiers, other troops being issued the Short Land Model. The haversack is of heavy tan linen fastened with three plain pewter buttons. The canteen is tin. *Katcher*

While an almost permanently established court martial began to impose a kind of discipline on the rebel force, and while the siege of Boston was maintained, a plan emerged for a Continental army. The volunteers would re-enlist under congressional authority instead of their individual colony; uniformly paid, supplied and administered by Congress, they would serve until the end of 1776. Strength was set at twenty-six infantry regiments of some 700 men each, one artillery regiment and one rifle regiment. Each infantry regiment would have eight companies each of four officers and eighty-six men. The new plan was not greeted warmly by the rebels. Officers who would now be down-graded protested hotly; men who insisted on serving in their own local units, under their own elected officers, simply went home. In December 1775 the Connecticut volunteers, despite every plea and encouragement that Washington could devise, declared that their original term of enlistment was up, and decamped en masse. By March 1776 Washington had 9,000 Continental troops, out of the 20,000 envisaged, and was forced to fill his ranks with short-term militia units, with all the attendant problems and anxieties. As serious as the manpower problem was the shortage of every military necessity; with some of his army armed with improvised spears, Washington was inevitably circumscribed in his conduct of offensive operations. Between the summer of 1775 and the following spring the position was slowly improved, particularly by the capture of British supply ships, the purchase of stores from French and Dutch colonies in the West Indies, and the arrival of Colonel Henry Knox with the artillery from Ticonderoga, brought east under appalling conditions.

Below
Reproduction—typical 'smallclothes' of the period, carefully copied from contemporary patterns. The basic design of knee-breeches, stockings, shirt, and sleeveless waistcoat was common to all nationalities. *Katcher*

Two hand-coloured engraved plates by Berger after Daniel Chodwiecki, published in 1784 by Haude und Spener of Berlin. They show: an 'American sharpshooter' in fringed linen coat, slouch hat. and overalls, carrying a German-style Jäger rifle: a member of the Pennsylvania Line, in the white-faced blue of the 1779 regulations: a trooper of 'General Washington's Mounted Lifeguard', with a white coat faced with blue,

1. *Americanischer Scharffschütz oder Jäger (Rifleman)*
2. *regulaire Infanterie von Pensylvanien.*

1. *General Washington's reitende Leibgarde.*
2. *die independent Company, Chef General Washing.*

buff breeches, and a black leather helmet decorated with a fox-tail and a red turban: and an officer of Washington's Independent Company, in white smallclothes, blue coat faced white, and gold lace. Note the white-on-black cockades, in honour of the French alliance. *Anna S. K. Brown Military Collection*

When Washington moved against Boston in March 1776 he profited from a British error of judgement – one of many. Howe, who now commanded, was justifiably unhappy at his cramped position; he therefore abandoned the city without a fight and shipped his forces to Halifax, Nova Scotia, leaving behind large quantities of everything Washington needed so desperately, including 250 cannon. This gain was balanced by an American misjudgement of equal scale, however. Since the previous September two forces of rebels, under Montgomery and Benedict Arnold, had been attempting to reach and capture Quebec before the small British forces in Canada could be reinforced. Everything imaginable had gone wrong with the expedition; commanders and men had shown great courage, but hardship, hunger, disease and desertion had reduced the survivors to ghosts by the time the plan was finally abandoned in the spring of 1776. This left New York vulnerable to a British attack from Canada.

In the southern colonies things went better for the rebels. Although there were considerable numbers of militant loyalists ('Tories') in Virginia and Carolina, Britain failed to support them in time, and they had been dispersed by rebel militia by the time a British expedition arrived off Charleston in June 1776. It was beaten off with quite heavy losses, and returned north to join forces with Howe, who was planning an attack on New York. The war had now lasted a year, and neither side could claim any important advantage; both bided their time while they feverishly built up forces equal to the tasks which confronted them. What those tasks would be was clarified on July 4th 1776, with the Declaration of Independence.

The colonies – now 'states' – jealously guarded their mutual independence, and the conduct of the war was to be bedevilled by their reluctance to grant the Continental Congress central powers to raise money or men. Congress could only set quotas for the states to fill in proportion to their resources quotas rarely met in manpower, and never in cash. The whole machinery of government was inadequate – hardly surprisingly – and Washington and the other rebel commanders suffered agonies of frustration as they attempted to make the 'jury-rig' administration work. To make matters worse, there was a lively fear in many Congressional circles that once entrusted with military power Washington or some other commander might seize personal power, and his efforts had sometimes to be devoted largely to allaying their fears whenever he applied for some new facility.

Little purpose would be served by describing in detail the see-saw campaigns of 1776 and 1777. They may be summarised briefly as examples of Washington's genius at holding together a caricature of an army in times of inactivity; at using it to its best ability to gain time; and at somehow maintaining his grip on affairs when his own occasionally serious military mistakes led to defeats. The summer of 1776 saw a series of defeats for the rebels around New York, defeats from which they were allowed to extricate themselves without paying the full price through a lack of 'follow-through' on the part of the British. December of that year saw the remnants of the rebel army retreating south-west across the Delaware in some disarray; but, confident that the little force could be crushed in the spring, Cornwallis put his British army into winter quarters rather than crossing into Pennsylvania and finishing the affair once and for all. Though decimated by desertion, sickness, and the stubborn withdrawal of short-term units, Washington's army continued to exist – to

Overleaf (left)
Reproduction—Continental sergeant in marching order. Colonel Hartley's Regiment of Foot Guards was raised around York, Pennsylvania, in 1776, and the white rose of the knapsack device is the emblem of the town. The black hat is decorated with false silver lace. The coat is blue with buff facings and is cropped rather short—coat-tails were often sacrificed for patching when uniforms showed hard wear. The red epaulette is a mark of rank, as is the 1742 pattern British army hanger, slung from the right shoulder in a buff waist belt; this is the pattern of sword most widely used by sergeants of all Revolutionary War armies. The bayonet scabbard for the 1774 Charleville is carried with the sword in a double frog. The cartridge box is brown leather, on a white cloth belt. The tin canteen is a local copy of the British pattern. *Katcher*

Overleaf (right)
Reproduction—a Continental officer of 1778,The hat is black with gold lace. The smallclothes are white, and include a 'belted waistcoat'. The coat is blue faced with buff, with the single left epaulette of a lieutenant. He carries an espontoon, and wears a British officers' sword slung on a buff belt with a brass plate. *Katcher*

such good effect that he managed to repair the shaky morale of the troops and public by crossing the Delaware again and winning a very stylish little victory over Hessian troops at Trenton on Boxing Day 1776. He then manoeuvred with some skill to avoid the heavy British counter-offensive, and got his tattered battalions safely into winter quarters.

At the turn of the year he began to build a new army yet again, armed with new Congressional powers to raise an army of 60,000 to serve for the duration of the war rather than for short fixed terms. By no means all the weaknesses of the system were eradicated, but with unprecedented dictatorial powers to appoint and dismiss, to commandeer and to levy, Washington had a chance. Nevertheless, the men who actually enlisted for the duration were always in a small minority, and Washington never had more than 10,000 under arms at any time during the campaigns of 1777. The use he could make of them was increased by an improving flow of supplies and arms from France, and the arrival of foreign experts as advisors and training officers. Some were mere adventurers, but others – men like Kosciuszko and Pulaski from Poland, du Portail and Lafayette from France, and above all Friedrich von Steuben from Prussia – were to be of enormous service to the rebel cause.

Throughout the spring and summer of 1777 Washington and Howe engaged in indecisive counter-manoeuvres in New Jersey. In August Howe embarked his army and sailed up Chesapeake Bay; his intention was a thrust at Philadelphia, the Continental capital. Troops under Lord Cornwallis neatly outflanked Washington's blocking position on the Brandywine River, and although the rebels managed to avoid envelopment the capital was occupied by the redcoats. Washington attacked the British position at Germantown, north of the

city, without success. Meanwhile British forces under Burgoyne had been advancing south from Canada, with the ultimate objective of Albany. Aided by Loyalists and Indians, the British had achieved considerable success around Lake Champlain and in the Mohawk Valley; the activities of the Indians in this latter campaign were to cause much hatred of the British for employing them against the colonists. Desperate delaying manoeuvres by the rebel commanders facing Burgoyne slowed him down to the point that he had to gamble on pushing ahead to Albany before winter fell, or face disaster; his supplies were failing and his intelligence as well – a bloody battle at Oriskany in August had so discouraged his Indians that many had melted away. Burgoyne, ever a gambler, decided to push on toward Albany with incautious haste; and in October, out-manoeuvred, blocked, eventually sur-rounded and starving, his army surrendered at Saratoga.

Although the winter of 1777-78 found the rebel armies still pitifully under strength and handicapped by the conflicting decisions of the states, Saratoga was to bring a priceless advantage to the colonists – beyond the simple achievement of the elimination of an important British force and the frustration of a manoeuvre which could have split the colonies in two. The news of Burgoyne's surrender prompted the French government to negotiate a treaty with the rebels which almost amounted to a declaration of war on Britain; and it was this French involvement, according to an official American history of the US Army, which was to be the decisive factor in the final victory of the rebels.

The winter of 1777-78 saw Washington encamped in the snow at Valley Forge, with an army of less than 6,000 men. Through the inadequacy of the various agencies of supply

this little force suffered appalling privation, and their perseverance under these hideous conditions has become a national epic. When the weather finally eased and supplies began to get through in something like adequate quantities, there arrived at Valley Forge one Baron von Steuben, an ex-staff officer of Frederick the Great's army, who had been persuaded by the French to offer his services to Washington. He inspected the Valley Forge encampment, and his report so impressed Washington that he was appointed Inspector General and instructed to work out a standard training programme for the Continental Army. Carefully and patiently, starting with a 'model company' which he instructed personally, von Steuben taught the raw soldiers the rudiments of professional skill. He evolved a simplified form of Prussian drill to suit local conditions. He looked into their needs, and set an example of care and concern for his men's welfare which had been lacking in many rebel officers. He enforced the proper care and correct use of weapons, and drilled the Americans in the best employment of the bayonet; a consistent feature of their performance up to this time had been a loss of morale when faced by British redcoats fighting with this unnerving weapon, which the British soldier understood thoroughly and used with terrible efficiency. By his patience, his thorough knowledge of his profession, and not least by his blistering profanity – the only English he knew was unprintable – von Steuben turned potential soldiers into actual soldiers.

France's entry into the war had altered the British position drastically. The whole Empire would have to be guarded against the growing strength of the French Navy. Howe's succes-sor, General Sir Henry Clinton, was stripped of some of his troops as dispositions to guard Canada, Florida and the West Indies were

'Committee of Public Safety' musket—locally made copy of the standard British Army long arm of the day, the 'Brown Bess'. This particular example has Maryland marks.
H. L. Peterson Collection

made. He was instructed to give up Philadelphia, and with 10,000 men began to march back to New York, followed by Washington, whose forces had again been built up to some 13,500 men – better trained and equipped men than he had ever led before. He attacked the British at Monmouth on June 27th; although his troops showed their new confidence with the bayonet the encounter was indecisive, largely due to the lack of determination displayed by the American General Charles Lee. This was the last general engagement in the northern colonies. Washington set up a defensive system screening New York, and although local actions were fought a stalemate descended on the northern front which lasted throughout the remainder of 1778 and the whole of 1779.

Switching their attention to the south, where Tory sympathy still offered a hope that the states might be won back to the Crown one by one, the British overran the thinly populated state of Georgia in the winter of 1778-79. Encouraged by this, and by successful raids on Virginia, they prepared to make a general advance on the rebel centre of Charleston. Washington had insufficient men to prevent the British army from moving south from New York, and when, in May 1780, Clinton's troops arrived at the port, it was surrendered to them by the rebel General Lincoln. This disaster cost the colonists more than 5,000 precious troops. A belated relief force was caught at Waxhaws by British cavalry under the brilliant and ruthless Colonel Tarleton, and slaughtered. Rebel efforts in the south now degenerated into a vicious guerilla war between patriots and loyalists. In June a small force from Washington's army arrived in North Carolina as a nucleus around which resistance might be built in the new and desperate situation which faced the colonists. Overconfidence by the commander, General

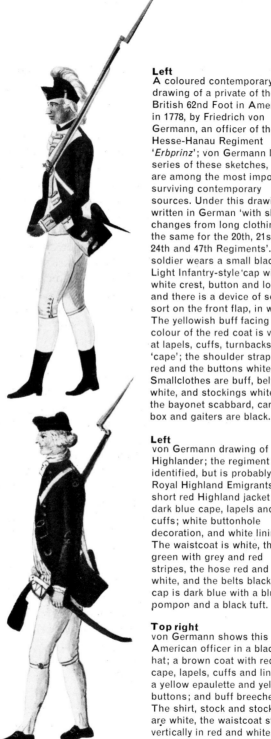

Left
A coloured contemporary drawing of a private of the British 62nd Foot in America in 1778, by Friedrich von Germann, an officer of the Hesse-Hanau Regiment *'Erbprinz'*; von Germann left a series of these sketches, which are among the most important surviving contemporary sources. Under this drawing is written in German 'with slight changes from long clothing, the same for the 20th, 21st, 24th and 47th Regiments'. The soldier wears a small black Light Infantry-style cap with a white crest, button and loop; and there is a device of some sort on the front flap, in white. The yellowish buff facing colour of the red coat is visible at lapels, cuffs, turnbacks and 'cape'; the shoulder strap is red and the buttons white. Smallclothes are buff, belts white, and stockings white; the bayonet scabbard, cartridge box and gaiters are black.

Left
von Germann drawing of a Highlander; the regiment is not identified, but is probably the Royal Highland Emigrants. The short red Highland jacket has a dark blue cape, lapels and cuffs; white buttonhole decoration, and white lining. The waistcoat is white, the kilt green with grey and red stripes, the hose red and white, and the belts black. The cap is dark blue with a blue pompon and a black tuft.

Top right
von Germann shows this American officer in a black hat; a brown coat with red cape, lapels, cuffs and lining, a yellow epaulette and yellow buttons; and buff breeches. The shirt, stock and stockings are white, the waistcoat striped vertically in red and white.

Gates, led to a crushing defeat at Camden in August; although the steadily improving Continental troops fought well they were hampered, and deserted, by the militia elements of the force, which fled from the bayonets of Cornwallis's redcoats and the sabres of Tarleton's cavalry.

Washington performed prodigies in holding his army together in the grim days of 1780. The unexpectedly long war had caused immense shortages and much disenchantment. The currency had depreciated until it was almost valueless, and the troops could not be paid, supplied, or equipped properly. The manpower problem was severe, despite the conscription of militiamen by the various states. There were mutinies in 1780 and 1781 which were only put down by the most ruthless methods.

Administrative reforms eased the preparations for one last burst of energy in 1781. Washington's recommendations for several key appointments were accepted and mobile forces were sent south to co-operate with rebel guerillas. In January 1781 the hated Tarleton was out-guessed and decisively beaten at Cowpens by Morgan's militia riflemen. Cornwallis reacted, and tried to speed the advance of his main force by abandoning much of his train; the rebel commander in the south, Nathaniel Greene, then led him on a long wild goose chase through the wilderness which reduced the British force to a sorry condition. A spoiling action at Guilford Court House in March cost Cornwallis heavy casualties, and Greene slipped away without attempting to hold his ground. Cornwallis led his deteriorating army back to the coast, and took command of all British troops in Virginia – some 7,000 men, about a third of the regulars in America. Eventually, on Clinton's instructions, Corn-

wallis established a single large base on the coast – at Yorktown, just off Chesapeake Bay.

Washington saw the chance for the final blow. Taking advantage of the announced intention of the French fleet to make a demonstration in Chesapeake Bay in the near future, and taking some 4,000 French troops under his command at Newport, he skilfully disengaged from Clinton and set out southwards. When the French ships arrived they landed another 3,000 men, and their presence effectively sealed off Yorktown from British naval assistance or evacuation. These new troops, and a prodigious recruitment from the local militia, brought Washington's strength up to more than 16,000 – giving him, at last, a local superiority over the British of well over two to one. The siege of Yorktown began, masterminded by French experts and planned on conventional European lines. On October 19th, 1781 Cornwallis surrendered.

For two more years Washington and Greene kept their armies in the field, and some minor actions in the south remained to be fought; but for all practical purposes Yorktown ended the War of Independence. The face-saving diplomatic negotiations over details of a treaty would drag on for weary months, but the final end was not in doubt. The vast American continent would no longer be merely the rich arena in which the nations of the Old World fought sideshows to their centuries-long struggle for power in Europe. It would be the birthplace of a new Republic, a social experiment unique in history. The course of that experiment was to prove so turbulent, however, that it was to be 135 years after Yorktown before foreign troops entered US territory under arms and killed American citizens for the last time.

16. Private of Grenadier Company, British 33rd Regiment of Foot, 1776

The 33rd Foot (in more recent years, the Duke of Wellington's Regiment, the only unit in the British Army named after a non-royal person) saw action during the War of Independence at Long Island and Harlem Heights, at Charleston, Camden, and King's Mountain, at Guilford Court House and Yorktown. A detachment is thought to have accompanied Burgoyne's expedition in 1777. The regiment was originally raised in 1702 as the Earl of Huntington's Regiment.

The grenadiers in any battalion were picked for their height and strength; tall caps – originally more practical than tricorns for men who had to throw grenades – added to their impressive appearance. The original mitre cap had by this stage given place to a similar style trimmed heavily with black fur; a black Japanned metal plate bore raised white metal decorations in the form of the Royal Arms and motto, and the bag of the cap was of red cloth. The hair was often fastened up under the back for convenience.

The red coat of this soldier has red facings and white lining; the regimental lace is white with a red line. Since 1768 the smallclothes of the infantry had been white or, in a few cases, buff. Woollen stockings are worn, with black cloth half-gaiters. The usual field equipment is carried, and in this case the crossbelt supporting the cartridge box is distinguished by a brass match-case – another reminder of the traditional equipment and function of the grenadiers.

17. Private, The Royal Greens, 1777

It is estimated that the call for Independence split the colonists in proportions of roughly two-thirds rebels, one-third loyalists; far from being in a tiny minority, the 'Tories' throughout the colonies totalled some 60,000 men. Some states had a loyalist majority, and numerous corps of loyalist troops were raised, some by the personal expenditure of prominent landowners and businessmen. The engagements which took place between loyalist and revolutionary were invariably fought out with more bitterness than those between revolutionary and British regular, and both sides are known to have inflicted atrocities on one another. Many of the loyalist units were of excellent quality, but their leadership and the degree of encouragement and support they received from the British armies left something to be desired. Prominent Tory corps included The Queen's Rangers, originally raised by Robert Rogers of Seven Years War fame; De Lancey's Brigade from New York; Butler's Rangers, a force of frontiersmen who acquired a ruthless reputation; Tarleton's British Legion; and other volunteer units raised in Maryland, Pennsylvania, the Carolinas, and New York.

New York was a centre of loyalist sentiments, and among the several Tory corps raised in the area was The Royal Greens; first raised by Sir John Johnson in 1776, this unit became The King's Royal Regiment of New York two years later. It was of regimental size, although the actual number varied quite widely during the course of the war; largely composed of men from isolated communities in upper New York state, the corps proved adept at backwoods fighting, and soon made a name for itself.

The uniform is of conventional cut, but in accordance with the general practice adopted when supplying loyalist units from 1776-1778, it is green rather than red. In 1778 most loyalist units received red uniforms in place of this pattern. Facing colours were various. (In the earliest stages of the war loyalist volunteers displayed as motley an appearance as their rebel enemies; most wore civilian clothing, and some colonists of Scots stock fought in their traditional national dress, complete with broadswords.) The Royal Greens used white facings, white waistcoats and breeches in the standard British Army pattern, and pewter buttons marked 'RP' for 'Royal Provincials'. Knee-length gaiters of brown cloth are reported to have been issued, and the normal British field equipment was worn. The brass hearts forming the fastening for the coat turn-backs are typical of the period. It is believed that a red hat cockade was a widely used loyalist emblem; in the manner of many 18th Century soldiers this Tory has replaced his cockade, lost or worn out, with a bunch of feathers, dyed to the appropriate colour. Belts and leather gear were often of buff rather than pipeclayed strapping.

18. Officer, 16th (Queen's) Light Dragoons, 1777

The only two British cavalry regiments sent to America during the Revolutionary War were the 16th and 17th Light Dragoons. The 16th had originally been raised by John Burgoyne, and he remained its Lieutenant-Colonel Commandant until his brief period in disgrace following his surrender at Saratoga. The regiment fought at Belle Isle in 1761 and distinguished itself in Portugal the following year. They were shipped to America in 1776, and fought in numerous actions. Most of these were minor ones, in keeping with the traditional tasks to which the mounted troops were committed, but the unit did particularly well at White Plains and Brandywine Creek. After suffering heavy losses the 16th was shipped home in 1778, many of its remaining effectives being transferred to the 17th Dragoons.

The officer illustrated here wears the stiff leather helmet with metal decorations worn by dragoons for the past twenty years. It has a brass-covered crest, a red plume, and a turban in the regimental facing colour of blue. The front plate bears an insignia based on the royal cypher. The red coat is faced in blue, as this was a royal regiment.

The rank and file wore very similar uniforms, with white lace replacing the silver worn by officers. The normal armament carried by Light Dragoons comprised a short flintlock carbine fastened to a shoulder belt by a snap-hook and ring, a sword, and a pair of pistols in saddle holsters.

19. Grenadier, Hesse-Hanau Musketeer Regiment Erbprinz, 1780

Since the British and Hanoverian monarchies were united early in the 18th Century Britain had on more than one occasion strengthened her position in an emergency by acquiring the services of German troops, both in and out of the United Kingdom itself. In the Revolutionary War Britain's total strength in regular troops was 33,000, a force inadequate to prosecute the war against the colonists, protect the home country, and guard against developments in her other overseas possessions. Accordingly various agreements were concluded which secured the services of large numbers of troops from Germany, mainly from the various provinces of Hesse; and in all some 40,000 German troops, collectively referred to by friend and foe alike as 'Hessians', served in America. At any one stage of the war roughly a third of the Crown forces in North America were German mercenaries; in this context the word mercenary is used literally, although the soldiers served in regular national regiments under their own officers.

The Hesse-Hanau Fusilier Regiment *Erbprinz* first landed at Quebec in June 1776, and fought at Ticonderoga, Freeman's Farm, Bemis Heights and Saratoga. In 1780 the designation was changed to 'Musketeer Regiment', and the uniform facings from rose pink to crimson. The regiment had a grenadier company throughout its career, notwithstanding the changed designation. The blue coat and white breeches were worn by most Hessian units, with different facing colours and waistcoats. The white metal plate of the grenadier cap bears the Hessian arms in an elaborate design, and the crimson and white pompon is a regimental distinction. The cartridge box, worn centrally on the front of the waistbelt, bears the cypher of the *Erbprinz* Wilhelm of Hesse. The rank and file traditionally wore moustaches while the officers were clean-shaven.

20. Jäger, Brunswick Light Infantry Battalion von Barner, 1777

The Duchy of Brunswick was a traditional supplier of hired troops to Britain, and a treaty was signed between the two in January 1776 whereby the Duchy agreed to provide a corps of just under 4,000 infantry and a regiment of dragoons for service in America. Among the infantry was the Light Infantry Battalion von Barner, commanded by an officer of that name, and mustering four light infantry and one *jäger* companies.

The Brunswick corps formed a major part of Burgoyne's ill-fated army in the Saratoga campaign of 1777. They were present at Ticonderoga, Hubbardton, Freeman's Farm and Bemis Heights, suffering heavy casualties at Bennington. More than 1,000 had become casualties before the survivors were boxed up at Saratoga. Among the best of 'Gentleman Johnny's' units was the Light Infantry Battalion von Barner, an élite force raised from among the foresters and hunting communities of the Duchy; they proved most adept at the type of backwoods fighting they found in America. The light infantry companies wore blue coats with black velvet collars and cuffs, the *jäger* company coats and waistcoats of forest green faced with red. The *jäger* illustrated here wears the buff leather breeches and gauntlets worn by all ranks. Officers and men alike were armed with hunting swords and rifles, with long cartridge boxes on the front of the belt. The weapons were often of excellent quality, personally purchased or presentation items, and the German foresters showed great skill with them. All ranks wore the aiguilette on the right shoulder, in silver for officers and in white for enlisted men; similarly, officers had silver rather than green sword-knots.

21. Colonial militiaman, 1775

No uniform regulations for the whole Continental Army were issued until 1779, and before that date – and in many cases, long after it – the revolutionary forces presented an extremely motley appearance. By far the greater number of the volunteers wore civilian dress throughout the war, and even the Line regiments were often forced to improvise through shortages and procurement difficulties. The importance of a common uniform was not lost on General Washington, but he had to make do with the material at his disposal.

The cocked hat, or any one of innumerable wide-brimmed hats, was the usual wear of the troops. Knitted caps, various felt or leather caps based on the Light Infantry cap of the day, and captured enemy hats were all worn in great numbers. The hunting shirt, illustrated here, was the preferred campaigning dress even if the wearer belonged to one of the few provincial units which was adequately provided with a specific uniform. Washington himself recommended it; it was practical, it could be worn over any other clothing in winter or next to the skin in summer without spoiling the vaguely military effect of a group of troops wearing it, and according to him its associations with hawk-eyed backwoods marksmen made British troops nervous as soon as they saw it. This militiaman carries his own gun, a heavy fowling piece, and his own powder horn and bullet bag, souvenirs of peacetime hunting expeditions. His few possessions are bundled into a rough linen knapsack slung high on his back by a strap over the shoulder.

22. Private, 1st Pennsylvania Battalion, 1776

The better state volunteer units contained at least some men dressed in uniforms chosen by the local militia, usually on the basis of cheapness and easy availability; these were of a wide variety of shades, but brown seems to have been highly favoured. When Washington began raising his Line regiments he made a virtue of necessity and laid down that brown coats should be the basis of the infantryman's uniform henceforward. A wide range of facing colours were used by the various states in outfitting their troops; often a coat would be the only item a man was issued, and he had to shift for himself in finding a hat, footwear and 'smallclothes' – ie breeches and waistcoat.

The soldier from Pennsylvania is in full dress – probably an extremely rare occurrence during

his career. The 1st Pennsylvania Battalion formed the nucleus for the formation of the 2nd Pennsylvania Regiment of the Pennsylvania Line of the Continental Army in October 1776. The usual hunting frocks or blanket coats were worn in the field, but for full dress the unit wore a brown coat faced with green; even so, some companies are reported to have been unable to procure this scheme and to have worn brown with buff, blue with red, or any other uniform coats they could lay their hands on. Buff-coloured breeches, white stockings, black spatterdashes and white leather equipment complete the uniform. The soldier carries a camp kettle of contemporary style.

23. Sergeant, 1st Connecticut Regiment, 1780

By 1779, after many false starts, supply failures, swindles by profiteers, and unfulfilled orders for uniform cloth from France and Holland, Washington managed to secure the approval of Congress for a single basic uniform for the infantry of the Continental Line. The idea of outfitting all troops in dark blue coats and white smallclothes, with a different facing colour for each of the thirteen states, had been abandoned; the difficulties of providing sufficient cloth of thirteen different colours were unsurmountable. By this stage dark blue was, *de facto*, the most widely used colour anyway, with brown faced with red probably second in popularity.

The troops were divided into groups, as follows. The infantry of New Hampshire, Rhode Island, Massachusetts and Connecticut would wear blue coats lined and faced with white. Those from New York and New Jersey would wear dark blue faced with buff, lined white. Pennsylvania and Delaware, Maryland and Virginia would wear red facings, lined white; and Georgia and the two Carolinas would wear dark blue faced with a lighter blue, the buttonholes taped with white and the linings white. White smallclothes were to be worn throughout; and breeches and stockings with spatterdashes were discouraged in favour of the overall trousers illustrated here, in varying weights and materials depending on the season. Rank would be indicated by white epaulettes for non-commissioned officers, and a system of single silver epaulettes for company officers. Sergeants carried swords in addition to their muskets and bayonets. Officers wore a red sash, a sword slung from a crossbelt, and carried a half-pike or espontoon – though the latter would have been abandoned in favour of a rifle, musket or fusil in action. The black cocked hats of the enlisted men were bound with white tape, in theory – it is highly unlikely that a soldier would give up a perfectly good hat because it lacked this refinement, and almost equally unlikely that he would hurry to add it in the middle of a campaign. The cockade became white-on-black in honour of the French alliance by about 1780-81. Infantry buttons were of white metal.

It must be emphasised that it probably took well over a year, if not longer, for the 1779 regulations to become reality. Under the circumstances of the day – the relative uncertainty of supply, the isolation of units from depots, the wide independence in many aspects of command enjoyed, and demanded, by individual leaders – there must have been many units which were disbanded in 1783 without having been fully equipped with the new uniforms, whose supply depended on state procurement.

24. Trooper, 4th Continental Dragoons, 1779
Washington's army was always critically weak in mounted troops, and in some actions – notably Brandywine Creek – the lack of cavalry 'eyes' had serious results. In 1777 Congress organised four regiments of Continental Cavalry on the British Light Dragoon model, comprising six troops of sixty men each. Bedevilled by the same supply shortages as the infantry, the cavalry were often hard put to it to mount twenty-five men in any troop, and the dragoons not infrequently fought as infantry. In addition to the Continental regiments there were various state units and, particularly in the south, some effective mounted militia formations. None of these units were committed to conventional European cavalry functions on any large scale, however, and scouting and courier duties represented their usual rôle.

The dress of Washington's mounted troops was as motley as that of the infantry. The four Continental regiments wore coats of conventional design, usually shorter in the tail than those of the infantry but not invariably so, with waistcoats, breeches and high boots. The normal headgear was a helmet, either of stiff leather or of brass, decorated with a plume or fur roach and sometimes with a turban. The 1st Continental Dragoons (Bland's) wore blue faced with red, the 2nd (Sheldon's), wore blue faced with buff, the 3rd (Baylor's) wore white faced with blue, and the 4th (Moylan's) wore, from 1779 onwards, green faced with red. The styles of

headgear and the colours of plumes and turbans were very varied and changed at least once for each regiment within the period of the war. Breeches were usually of buff-coloured leather.

The sword was the normal weapon of the patriot cavalry, both from policy and from the constant shortage of firearms; more than a dozen different styles of sabre are known to have been in use, and distinctions between them are irrelevant. Pistols were carried in saddle holsters or belt-hooks, but carbines were as rare as gold. No carbines are known to have been manufactured in the colonies at this time, and patriot troopers relied on cut-down muskets, captured British carbines and musketoons, imported French carbines (such as the weapon which the trooper in the illustration has just received, with incredulous joy!) and even full-size muskets. At one time General Washington looked with favour on the idea of equipping the Continental cavalry with blunderbusses, but nothing is thought to have come of the plan.

25. Fusilier, French Infantry Regiment Soissonais, 1780-83
Apart from the helpful manoeuvres of the French fleet, the revolutionary forces were directly aided in the War of Independence by French regular troops. The Comte de Rochambeau's expeditionary force landed at Newport, Rhode Island in June 1780, and eventually saw action around New York before marching south to take part in the seige of Yorktown; among the units of this force were the regiments of *Bourbonnais, Royal Deux-Ponts, Soissonais,* and *Saintonge,* and the Irish and Polish mercenaries of Lauzun's Legion. The *Agénois, Gâtinois, Touraine, Armagnac, Cambrésis, Champagne, Auxerrois* and several other regiments also provided drafts when Admiral d'Estaing gathered another expeditionary force from French garrisons in the West Indies.

This fusilier of the *Soissonais* Regiment wears the smart new uniform and equipment authorised under the French army regulations of 1779. The coat, waistcoat and breeches are white, with the crimson facings of the seventh class of regiments; the sixty line regiments were grouped into ten classes of six regiments, each class with one facing colour. The regiments were also individually numbered, and *Soissonais* bore the number 41 on its yellow metal buttons. The regiment was made up mainly of

fusilier companies, with grenadier and chasseur (light) companies distinguished by variations of epaulettes and turn-back decorations. Fusiliers were not issued with swords, and unlike the other two types of troops wore only one crossbelt, supporting both the cartridge box and the bayonet. The knapsack is of unshaven cowhide, and this soldier still follows the old practice of carrying his water in a gourd. Black cloth gaiters were worn for campaigning, and white for full dress. Non-commissioned officers were distinguished by a system of cuff stripes or half-chevrons.

The crimson facings of the regiment's uniform are believed to have faded quickly in America, as contemporary accounts speak of them as pink.

The regiments which sailed from Brest were armed with the Model 1777 musket, while those drafts collected from Martinique and Guadeloupe carried earlier models.

PLATE 4

16

18

19

17

20

PLATE 5

21

23

24

22

25

3 The Confusions of Victory

The American victory in the Revolutionary War saw the birth of a myth which was to cause the young nation endless difficulty for almost a century, a myth which did not finally die until the Battle of First Bull Run in the opening months of the Civil War. This canard, which took firm root in the public mind, was made the more dangerous by the basic disunity of the states once the common threat of British oppression was removed. It may be termed the Volunteer Syndrome, and its essentials may be stated thus:

A standing army is a threat to civil liberty and a negation of everything for which the Republic stands. Each state should have complete control over the levying of troops among its citizens, and over the financial provisions which must be made for the equipment and support of those troops. No state troops should have to serve under a commander from another state, who may use their lives and the taxes of their state to further the interests of his own. The victory over Britain proves that standing armies are not necessary, anyway. In the event of danger once more threatening the nation as a whole – a fact which the individual states will accept only after the most searching and lengthy deliberations – the sturdy citizens will simply leave their ploughs, take up long rifle and hunting shirt, and take to the woods for a strictly limited period, to trounce the foe before the harvest is due. They will then disperse, saving their states any further anxiety over money, the necessity to make decisions, or the undesirable presence of bodies of armed men not answerable to the state authorities.

The absurdities of this myth need no emphasis. In the event, the states often allowed danger to overwhelm other states without lifting a finger to go to their aid. The volunteer was usually unwilling, and when a physical threat to his own community actually forced

Reproduction—a private of the 16th US Infantry in the uniform of 1814. The coatee is the old type with red collar and cuffs; officially superceded by the all-blue type in 1813, it was certainly worn after that date. The decoration is in white wool-worsted tape or 'lace'; note that there are four buttonholes on the cuffs, only three of which show from this angle. White duck trousers are worn over black half-gaiters and black laced shoes. The black leather 1813 model shako has the white plume and cord of the infantry. The 'lower' of the white crossbelts supports a black leather cartridge box behind the right hip; the 'upper' one, with a plain brass plate, supports the socket bayonet for the 1812 Springfield musket, a copy of the Charleville. The wooden canteen slung on the left hip is painted light blue, as is the canvas knapsack. The coatee has very long-cut sleeves; and note the white lining showing at the turn-backs. *Katcher*

Rear view of a US infantryman of the War of 1812, in full field equipment. *Artist's Collection*

him into the field his effectiveness was very questionable. His officers were elected from among locally important businessmen and landowners, and usually lacked even the rudiments of sound military education. The periodic musters and drills degenerated into an excuse for a jug-party. Most important of all, the lessons so patiently instilled by von Steuben were forgotten by all but a handful. It was not the keen-eyed rifleman who had won America her independence, but the drilled, ordered ranks of the Continental Line. The sniper in the thicket can harass a conventional army, but he cannot drive it from the field. That requires the big battalions.

The process of degeneration of American arms began before the treaty with Britain was even ratified. The detailed negotiations took until 1783, and in the meantime the army, its pay in arrears and its camps stirred by conflicting rumours, began to seethe with discontent. It was finally paid off late that year, with the question of a peacetime army still undecided. At one stage the Congress authorised residual guard troops for arsenals totalling exactly 87 officers and men. It was finally agreed that a single regiment of eight infantry and two artillery companies be retained, with a strength of about 700. By the end of 1784 only some 400 were under arms; New Jersey, Pennsylvania, New York and Connecticut had been called upon to provide drafts, but only the first two had responded. The pattern was beginning to emerge. The under-strength force was commanded by Lieutenant-Colonel Josiah Harmar of Pennsylvania.

Civil unrest, which led at one point to a rebellion which had to be put down by force, went hand in hand with repeated deadlocks over the questions of finance and autonomy until about 1790. Unrest on the frontiers finally led to the establishment of a force which

varied between 5,000 and 6,000 men in the
period 1792-96. The most important incidents
of this period were the defeat of Harmar, the
massacre of St Clair, and the victory of
Wayne's Legion.

It was decided in June 1790 that trouble-
some Indians in Ohio must be given a lesson
in accordance with the dignity of the Republic;
Harmar was consequently given command of
a motley force including some 300 of the tiny
regular army and about 1,400 militia from
Pennsylvania and Kentucky. He led them
through the wilderness from Cincinnati to
what is now Ft Wayne, Indiana. It proved
impossible to instil any discipline among the
volunteers, who tended to scatter at their own
whim. After two small parties had been badly
mauled in ambushes Harmar led his sorry
command back to Cincinnati. Worse was to
come.

The following year Congress decided to try
again, and Arthur St Clair, Governor of the
North-West Territory and newly breveted
General, was authorised to raise a second
regular infantry regiment and 2,000 volunteers,
the latter for a period of six months. Even by
delaying the campaign for two months beyond
the planned date St Clair was unable to find
2,000 volunteers. In September 1791 he finally
left Cincinnati with 600 regulars and 1,400
militia, and marched north. On November 3rd,
encamped for the night some hundred miles
from the town, the force was rushed by about
1,000 Indians. Panic ensued, and after about
900 casualties had been suffered the survivors
withdrew in disorder.

The lesson got home at last. Congress
authorised two more regular infantry regiments
and one mixed unit of infantry and dragoons,
and gave command to the able 'Mad Anthony'
Wayne, leader of the Pennsylvania Line and
hero of Stony Point. In three years of hard

The 'Waterloo' pattern shako of a British infantryman of the period, with false front and brass plate; it retains its plume but the cord had been misplaced. Some of the British regiments which landed in America wore this shako; others, shipped from foreign posts rather than from England or France, still wore the old 'stovepipe' shako. *Hinton/Robson*

his men into professional competence. He did not commit them to battle until he had tried to negotiate a settlement with the Indians; their reply was a vigorous attack on Fort Recovery in 1794. This was decisively beaten off, and the victory raised the morale of the Legion at just the right time; confident and eager, the compact little army advanced once again. In August the campaign was brought to a successful climax at the Battle of Fallen Timbers. Wayne sent his legionaries and his screen of mounted militia scouring through the countryside burning crops and destroying villages, and then withdrew in good order to Cincinnati. The cowing of the Indians coincided with various long-delayed international agreements which led to the withdrawal of the last British frontier posts in the northern interior of the States.

The Legion structure was abandoned in 1796. The following year the force available to Congress comprised four regiments of infantry, two companies of dragoons, and the Corps of Artillerists and Engineers which totalled about four battalions; in all some 3,000 men, of whom rather more than half were scattered in small detachments along the southern and western frontiers, and the remainder watched the Canadian border. The first of the wars between Britain and revolutionary France caused widespread tension and some expansion of American forces, to the tune of an artillery regiment and the first regiment of Marines. During the period of uncertainty a 'Provisional Army' was authorised, of twelve infantry and one cavalry regiments raised for the duration of the crisis. When this army was finally disbanded in June 1800 some 4,000 men had been assembled and had received between six and twelve months training – a useful investment for the future.

The standing army was progressively cut

work Wayne forged his 'Legion' – as the regular army was now entitled – into an effective force organised along surprisingly modern lines. It was divided into four Sub-Legions, each of which was a self-sufficient combat group comprising two infantry and (in the 1st and 2nd Sub-Legions only) one rifle battalions, a company of artillery and a troop of dragoons, the whole commanded by a brigadier-general. Wayne led his Legion along roughly the same line of advance as his unhappy predecessors, but travelled slowly and secured his rear with a line of forts and block-houses. He went into winter quarters, and used every hour to drill

The gilt metal officer's gorget was a feature of British uniform for a long period. The example on the left, with the wreathed Royal Cypher, was introduced early in the 19th Century and would have been worn during the War of 1812; the gorget on the right, with the Royal Arms, is the earlier type in use during the Revolution.

back over the next few years, to a figure of some 3,000; but although the cavalry disappeared altogether the ratio of trained artillery was much increased, and the general quality was superior to that of a few years previously. This level was maintained until the War of 1812. Important innovations included the foundation of the West Point Military Academy, initially under the aegis of the Artillerists and Engineers but soon the fount of up to date instruction in all the military sciences. (At this stage the two technical branches were separated once more, becoming the Corps of Engineers and the Regiment of Artillerists.) This first step towards creating a professional elite within the nation, rather than continuing to rely on foreign experts, was a milestone on the road to military excellence.

One of the crises which occurred during this period was the confrontation between settlers pushing westwards and the confederation of Indians led by Tecumseh of the Shawnee. William Harrison, Governor of the Indiana Territory and later President, put to the Secretary of War a plan for a pre-emptive attack on the Indians. This was approved, and in September 1811 Harrison led a force northwards from Vincennes, comprising about 300 regular infantry and some 650 militiamen. At Tippecanoe, the main Indian encampment, Harrison pitched camp and held a conference with Tecumseh's brother; the great chief was absent at the time. At dawn the Indians attacked without warning. Harrison's men managed to beat off the attack with some difficulty, and launched a counter-charge which

The weapon of the redcoats—the ubiquitous 'Brown Bess', the smoothbore India Pattern musket. This example was made about 1800.

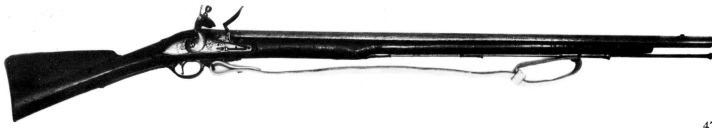

47

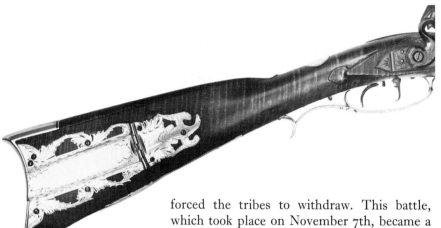

In contrast to the functional simplicity of the British musket, a detail view of a 'Kentucky rifle' of the period. This weapon, which actually owed its birth to German and Swiss immigrants in Pennsylvania, has entered folklore as the favoured weapon of the hawk-eyed American backwoodsman. These beautiful and deadly examples of the gunsmith's art were used by volunteers in the War of 1812; a frequent feature of the more highly decorated pieces was an elaborately fashioned brass patch-box lid in the butt. This fine example is by John Vogler of Salem, NC; it dates from around 1810. *Private collection*

forced the tribes to withdraw. This battle, which took place on November 7th, became a famous incident in Western folklore. Neither the expedition, nor the burning of the Indian village which followed the battle, can be seen as very creditable today; but there is no doubt that the little force of whites fought with great courage. Harrison's casualties were about forty dead and 150 wounded; Tippecanoe also cost America any chance of reaching terms with Tecumseh. When he found out about the defeat and destruction which had taken place in his absence the great Shawnee left his hunting grounds and took his warriors north, placing himself under the protection of British guns on the Canadian border.

The War of 1812 may be seen as 'unfinished business'. In some English minds the outcome of the War of Independence was less than decisive – incredible, but in keeping with contemporary attitudes which found it unthinkable that a mutiny against the Crown could be allowed to succeed. There were several causes of immediate friction, not least the extremely free hand British naval officers were allowed in their dealings with American shipping. Britain was locked in a death-struggle with Napoleon, and some American leaders thought the time was ripe for an invasion of Canada, long a source of irritation;

there were those who objected violently to the presence of the Union Jack anywhere on the continent.

The war was visibly approaching when, in January 1812, Congress voted a major increase in the regular army; this had an effective strength of some 7,000 infantry, riflemen, dragoons and artillery. The expansion authorised totalled 27,500 men – thirteen regiments – and a muster of 50,000 volunteers. Needless to say only a small fraction of this number had actually joined the colours by the time war broke out in June 1812. The army had a total strength of about 11,800 at that time, of whom some 5,000 were raw recruits. Counting regulars, the excellent Canadian militia regiments, potential civilian volunteers and Tecumseh's 3,500 Indians, the Crown could contemplate an effective force of about 20,000 on Canadian soil.

American attitudes to the new war varied sharply, and underlined the unreadiness of the disunited states for such an enterprise. Some states were utterly opposed to the war, and made no move to supply troops or support of any kind. Others responded apathetically, with too little, too late. New England, in particular, evinced almost complete disinterest; privateers sailed from New England ports on profitable expeditions, but on the land no effort was made. It was for this reason that the obvious invasion route towards Montreal and the heart of populated Canada was ignored, and the early campaigns took shape along the borders of the more enthusiastic western states, around the Great Lakes. Enthusiasm proved to be no substitute for experienced leaders and trained men, however, as the fighting on the Detroit and Niagara Rivers demonstrated.

Governor Hull moved up to the Detroit River with some 1,800 men, crossed it, manoeuvred indecisively, and was sent packing by the British General Brock with 700 regulars and 600 Indians; Hull promptly surrendered Detroit's defences to the enemy. Stephen van Rensselaer, with a force of a few regulars, some New York volunteers of unreliable temper, and the useless General Smyth as commander, was repulsed with heavy losses at Queenstown Heights; the only benefit from the action was that it caused the death of General Brock, killed leading a British counter-charge.

The year 1813 saw a number of clashes around the Lakes, from which America emerged victorious after Perry's naval victory on Lake Erie and Harrison's victory on the Thames River, which latter was largely due to the mounted militia from Kentucky – thus demonstrating that the one feature of volunteers on which one could count was their unpredict-ability. The Thames River victory also saw the death of the formidable Tecumseh and the break-up of his confederation. America's more favourable position was balanced out at the end of the year, however, by the disastrous failure of a two-pronged expedition against Montreal, largely due to the complete lack of mutual confidence or co operation exhibited by the commanders of the two columns. In March 1814 another assault on Canada comprising 4,000 men under General Wilkinson was repulsed at the Richelieu River by a mere two hundred redcoats backed by some small gun-boats. The patchy performance of the Ameri-can leaders and the American volunteers, ranging from dashing and brilliant to con-temptible, had become obvious, and in future command would be given increasingly to able young colonels of proven competence, rather than to political appointees or the preferred choices of the individual states. The new regiments slowly improved their performance,

While not of the highest quality, these photographs are important for the rarity of the subject—a genuine example of a US Infantry officer's coat of 1812-13. It was worn by Captain John Ellis Wool of the 13th US Infantry. It is basically dark blue, with red collar and cuffs, white turn-backs and silver decoration. This comprises collar lace, the edges of the small left shoulder strap, and loops on the right shoulder to hold the single silver epaulette of captain's rank, unfortunately missing here. At the join of the turnbacks are two small red diamonds outlined with silver lace. *Rensselaer County Historical Society*

49

The plated button of 'Wool's coat, nearly an inch across, have had the number of the regiment stamped in after manufacture. *Rensselaer County Historical Society*

though their supply organisation would leave much to be desired throughout the war. Men like George Izard, Winfield Scott and Jacob Brown began to make a name for themselves; it was Brown who gave America her first really significant land victory at Chippewa in July 1814. Later in the same month Brown's and Scott's troops suffered terrible losses at Lundy's Lane, but so did the redcoats; it was the hardest-fought and bloodiest battle of the war. Both sides fought with great courage and determination, and both claimed the victory.

The summer of 1814 was to live in legend for the landing in the Patuxent River of 4,000 British regulars led by General Ross. About half this force managed to disperse a hastily-assembled and unready army of some 6,000 Americans at Bladensburg in late August; whereupon Ross followed up his advantage by marching into Washington, burning down the White House and the Capitol, and withdrawing unmolested. The disgrace was wiped out the following month when the Maryland militia successfully fought off the same British force, which was advancing on Baltimore, and killed Ross himself; and almost simultaneously the British suffered an important defeat on Lake Champlain. British public opinion was growing sick of the war, which seemed a pointless side-show to a nation concentrating on the twenty-year struggle against Napoleon, now – apparently – reaching a victorious close.

The disenchantment turned to dismay in January 1815, when for reasons best known to himself General Sir Edward Packenham sent his superb Peninsula veterans marching over open ground on a narrow front against Andrew Jackson's cannon and riflemen before New Orleans. 'Ned' Packenham, a well-loved commander who had learned his trade – inadequately – under the great Wellington in Spain,

paid for his folly with his life; so did far too many of his tragically wasted infantry. Some 6,000 of them marched steadily into the killing-ground in front of the barricades where Jackson's 4,500 militia and heavy artillery support waited for them. More than 2,000 redcoats became casualties; and the man who took over command when Packenham fell released them from their futile courage and withdrew them to their camps. Had he not done so, the outcome of the battle might have been very different; a certain Colonel Thornton had led a small force of British infantry on to the west bank of the river, where they smashed through the American positions, overran a battery and put Jackson's entire line in jeopardy. But even if a victory had been gained to lay on the graves of the slaughtered redcoats, it would have been a pointless one; when the unshaken ranks of Highlanders and county infantry fell before Jackson's cannon, the Treaty of Ghent was already three weeks old. They died in peacetime.

The war was beneficial to America in many ways, not least in bringing to public attention men of the calibre of Jackson and Winfield Scott. It did not lead to any immediate and deepseated reforms in the areas of military activity where America was most deficient. The public took New Orleans to their hearts, and sang merry songs about the homespun militia, and the British 'running like Hell'. The British did not run like Hell; and their conduct under a murderous fire had been of a quality which no unit in all North America could have equalled. There were a few far-sighted officers in republican blue who ignored the merry songs and applied themselves to building the sort of professional spirit which could sustain men so tormented; but only a few.

PLATES 6,7,8

26. Drummer, New Jersey Infantry, 1782
Following the common practice of the day, this musician wears a coat in which the colours are the reverse of those worn by his comrades in the ranks. The coat is in buff, the facing colour of New Jersey regiments, and is faced with dark blue. The blue shoulder straps are also a peculiarity of musicians' uniforms. The coat is lined with buff rather than the normal white, and another New Jersey and New York distinction is the use of yellow instead of white metal buttons, with a 'USA' cypher. The peaked musician's cap of jacked leather is bound with white tape, and the usual ribbon cockade is fixed by a gold loop with a yellow metal button marked with an 'NJ' cypher. The white smallclothes are conventional.

27. American infantryman, 1786
An order of December 1782 had standardised the dress of all infantry units, irrespective of state origins, as a dark blue coat lined with white and faced with scarlet. It is unlikely in the extreme, however, that in the period between January 1783 and the disbandment of the army at the end of that year the states would have gone to the expense and trouble of re-clothing their men. The first American army to follow the regulation was probably the tiny force of 1784, in which the artillery companies were distinguished by red coat linings and yellow metal buttons, as well as by certain gold lace distinctions on officers' dress.

In the late 1780s the men of the small standing force saved their uniform coats by wearing, for normal drill and duties, a short fatigue jacket of the type illustrated here. The jacket might be tailored new, or cut down by the company tailors from old uniform coats, in which case they might retain the red cuffs. The black cocked hat with its white tape and black ribbon cockade is conventional, as are the white vest and 'overall' breeches and the pipe-clayed crossbelts supporting cartridge box and bayonet. The brush and pricker – for cleaning fouling from the lock of the flintlock musket – are carried on a fine brass chain from a convenient buttonhole.

28. Artillery Matross, 1791
The two companies of artillery which, with eight infantry companies, made up Josiah Harmar's First American Regiment, in 1784-86, were commanded by William Ferguson and John Doughty, and hailed from Pennsylvania and New York respectively. Doughty's New York company was originally raised by Alexander Hamilton in 1776, and could thus claim a uniquely unbroken lineage to Revolutionary days. Late in 1786 Congress, alarmed by the civil disturbances which culminated in the bloodshed of 'Shay's Rebellion' in Massachusetts, authorised a hasty expansion, including the formation of a Battalion of Artillery.

Doughty became Major Commandant of Artillery, and two extra companies were raised in Massachusetts and eventually sent south to guard the border with Spanish Florida. In 1791 the two original companies served in the Ohio territory, and late in that year they were almost wiped out in the St Clair disaster, losing both commanders and the bulk of the men to the arrows of the Miamis. The new companies were recalled from Georgia and a hastily rebuilt battalion, much below establishment, served with Wayne's Legion in 1794, and shortly thereafter they were absorbed into the new Corps of Artillerists and Engineers.

This Matross, illustrated in the act of paying the price of serving under St Clair, wears the standard pattern blue coat with red facings. His branch of service is indicated by the red lining of the coat, the brass buttons, and the yellow tape decorating his cocked hat. There was a noted shortage of white overalls, and blue were issued instead.

29. Infantryman, 1st Sub-Legion, 1794
This victor of Fallen Timbers wears a uniform entirely in keeping with the 1779 regulations, with the exception of his hat. The broad-brimmed 'slouch' with its dashing roach of bearskin is known to have been issued to company officers and men of the Legion some time between 1792 and 1794. The men had the brim decorated with coloured tape indicating their Sub-Legion – white for the 1st, red for the 2nd, yellow for the 3rd and green for the 4th. Cockades, plumes, and turbans were added for formal occasions. There is some confusion over the period and conditions of issue of a jacked leather Light Infantry style cap, with the same unit distinctions, which the Legion certainly wore at some stage of its life.

Officers and sergeants carried pole-arms in action – to help them with the ordering of their ranks, rather than as weapons – and wore red sashes and swords, with a single white crossbelt with an oval brass plate for commissioned ranks. Typical rank insignia of the day were a single right epaulette in worsted for a corporal, two worsted epaulettes for a sergeant, a single left bullion epaulette for a subaltern and a single right bullion epaulette for a captain, and bullion epaulettes on each shoulder for field officers. Generals still wore the Revolutionary general's uniform of a blue coat faced and lined buff, with buff smallclothes.

30. Dragoon, 3rd Sub-Legion, 1794
The cavalry troops which provided scouts, couriers, outriders and a small force of 'shock troops' for each Sub-Legion wore a shortened version of the conventional scarlet-faced blue coat. The leather dragoon caps had the same bearskin roach and coloured turbans and plumes as the infantry units' headgear. Riding boots and breeches replaced the overalls and shoes of the infantry, and a single crossbelt supported the sabre. A haversack and canteen were worn on campaign, on shoulder belts. When not actually in the field a high standard of 'spit and polish' was demanded of Wayne's Legion, and powdered hair would be the order of the day for all troops.

31. Spanish Cuera Dragoon, 1790s
The 'leather dragoons' were the frontier police of Spain's old American possessions. Throughout the 18th Century they patrolled, explored, escorted, scouted, and rode in punitive columns which set out from the chain of small forts running from the Gulf of Mexico to northern California. When Mexico became independent in 1823 it did not mean the end of the Mexican-based companies of this tough *gendarmerie*; it seems that they simply changed their red-yellow-red hat cockades for green-white-red, and soldiered on. They were apparently entitled to keep their arms and equipment when their six-year enlistment was over, and one source states that their unique armour was still to be seen around the small towns of California well into the middle years of the 19th Century.

This padded armour is obviously the most remarkable feature of the *Cuera* soldier. It was made by quilting six or seven thicknesses of hide, and was an imitation of the quilted cotton arrow-proof clothing encountered among various American peoples by the early Spanish pioneers in the 17th Century. Leather leggings, usually allowed to hang down and tied at the knee, protected the legs against scrub and thorns; when mounted the soldier sometimes wore extra leather aprons fixed to the belt, which hung over his legs and also provided some protection for the horse. At this date the hat, of traditional Spanish shape, was undecorated; in the early 19th Century it was turned up on one side and acquired a national cockade. The hair was worn long, and a kerchief was tied round the head under the hat. A simple uniform of blue with red collar and cuffs and protective leather inserts on the legs was worn as normal dress; a more elaborate parade dress appeared in later years. A leather shield, either oval or heart-shaped, was usually carried, decorated with the painted arms of Spain. The waistbelt supports a short, heavy sword; the crossbelt, embroidered with the name of the dragoon's base fort, supports a cartridge box with 24 loads for the flintlock carbine. The armament was completed by a pair of pistols and a six-foot lance.

32. Matross, 3rd New York Artillery, 1808
International tension in 1806, and an incident off their coast, prompted the New York authorities to enlarge their volunteer militia. This was already quite a prosperous and flourishing body, as often happened in the relatively wealthy urban centres; the local commercial and land-owning 'aristocracy' took an interest and spent money on uniforms and equipment out of a sense of civic pride. Two regiments of artillery already existed, and an autonomous battalion. To this latter was added a newly-raised battalion of four companies, to form a third regiment. At this time the first battalion of any regiment drilled with the actual cannon, and the second with muskets, as infantry. A soldier of the second battalion is illustrated.

His immense and unwieldy *chapeau bras* is worn diagonally, forward at the right hand side; this is so that he will not knock it from his head when he performs the 'shoulder arms'. Cannoneers wore theirs straight across the head. The usual style of artillery coat is worn, with scarlet lining and facings and yellow metal buttons. The short coatee was already coming into use, but it was to be some time before it became general wear. Blue overalls were usually worn for drill with the cannon, and white for infantry drill. Crossbelts of both black and pipe-clayed leather were used. The muskets were privately purchased.

52

33. Private, Spanish Regimiento de Infanteria de Luisiana, Florida, 1790s
The dwindling fortunes of imperial Spain were reflected in the degeneration and eventual loss of her American colonies. In 1762 France had ceded most of her possession of Louisiana to Spain; the French-speaking inhabitants resented being used as a pawn in an international chess game, and Spain was forced to raise and station troops in the new colony. An accommodation between Spanish rule and French culture was reached, and by the time the Revolutionary War broke out Spain was able to send her Louisiana Regiment into action against the British posts in Florida. The regiment was present at several battles between 1779 and 1781. In 1800 Spain returned Louisiana to France; her proprietorship had been in little more than name for many years. Three years later Napoleon, concerned with financing his European wars rather than with theoretical overseas possessions in a far-off continent, sold Louisiana to the United States for fifteen million dollars. The Spanish Louisiana Regiment kept its name, however, and continued to serve Spain in the Two Floridas until they too were passed over to the United States by a treaty of 1819.

The soldier illustrated is suffering the heat of the Everglades in a uniform of Bourbon white, made from locally produced cotton; this was as much a comment on the inability of Spain to supply her colonies as on the climate. The blue collar and cuffs are detachable for laundering purposes. The white vest and breeches are also of cotton, and the gaiters, held by buttons and knee-straps, are canvas. The crossbelts, and the sling of the 1752-model flintlock musket, are locally made of natural buff buckskin; conventional cartridge boxes and bayonets were issued. The hair would be powdered for parades and formal duties.

34. Sergeant of United States Infantry, 1813
The details of the changes in American army uniforms in the years immediately prior to the War of 1812 are somewhat obscure. The coat was replaced by the coatee, initially blue with red collar and cuffs, and in some cases with white tape 'blind buttonholes' across the chest. Some sources state, however, that shortcomings in the supply departments led to the appearance of black and grey coatees alongside the blue pattern. At any event, by the second year of the war a standard pattern seems to have emerged, and is illustrated here. The

blue collar is decorated with white tape, but the front is plain. The two white silk epaulettes are the rank insignia of a sergeant. (Other rank insignia of the period were a single white right epaulette for corporals, a single silver left epaulette for subalterns, a single silver right epaulette for captains, and two silver epaulettes for field officers.)

The shako is the leather pattern of 1813, very reminiscent of the British 'Waterloo' pattern with its high false front; this replaced the short-lived 1812 issue, of much the same design but in felt – this did not wear well in the field. The shako, distinguished by a white plume and cords for infantry personnel, was worn by both company officers and men. Officers' shakos had silver cords. The fatigue trousers worn by this NCO are another reminder of the lack of unified procurement and issue in the hasty expansions of 1812; troops went into action in trousers of many shades of grey, blue and brown, depending upon local availability, with or without spatterdashes. The red sash and straight sword carried in addition to the musket and bayonet are another indication of sergeant's rank; officers carried sabres. The long sleeves of the coatee are mentioned in contemporary sources; apparently they were prone to drastic shrinkage, and were deliberately tailored long for this reason.

35. Company officer, Glengarry Light Infantry Fencibles; Canadian militia, 1813
When Britain first acquired Canada in the aftermath of the Seven Years War, the uncertain loyalty of the predominantly French-speaking population was a cause for unease. By the War of 1812, however, this grudging acceptance of British rule had matured into a robust loyalty. Thousands of pioneers of British and allied stock had settled in the country, altering the racial balance; large numbers of hardy Scots, and ex-Loyalist veterans of the War of Independence, provided an underpinning for Canadian society and a nucleus for a vigorous militia movement. Britain had copied Imperial Rome, by offering land in Canada as an inducement to various classes of enlistees; these veteran *colonia* now sent their sons to ward off the threatened invasions from the south.

There were many different types of volunteer unit, their complex titles meaningless today but at the time defining the different conditions of service. There were Sedentry Militia and Select Incorporated Militia, Fencible Infantry and

Embodied Militia, Royal Veteran Battalions, and a host of others. Most were uniformed in the style of the British Line of the day, in brick-red coatees with different coloured facings at collar, shoulder and cuff, and white or grey trousers. The shakos worn were of both the 1800 'stovepipe' and 1812 'Waterloo' patterns. The usual equipment of the British army was issued – cartridge box and socket bayonet supported on white crossbelts, wooden or tin canteens, and the ubiquitous 'Brown Bess' musket. Locally made packs and haversacks were often worn in the field, however, and hide or fur sometimes replaced the normal canvas in these items.

The smart Glengarry Light Infantry Fencibles wore a uniform based closely on a British élite regiment of the day – the 95th Rifle Regiment, the famous 'Light Bobs' of the Peninsular War. The unit was raised in 1812 and served until 1816, seeing action in several battles including the bloody fighting at Lundy's Lane in July 1814, where the Glengarries distinguished themselves. They enlisted for three years, or the duration of the war, whichever was the shorter, and received cash bounties and the promise of one hundred acres of prime Crown land on completion of their service; the men received issue uniforms, though officers no doubt purchased theirs privately in the usual manner. The company officer illustrated here has an elegant tunic of Rifle cut, dark green with black facings, much silk frogging, and the three rows of silver buttons typical of this corps. His shako badge is the silver bugle-horn which distinguished the British Light units, in this case without any other decoration. The red officer's sash worn over the right shoulder rather than the left or the waist is a unit peculiarity; in the Line regiments it was worn round the waist and in Highland units over the left shoulder, but the Glengarries classed themselves both as Highlanders and as riflemen, and the Rifle officer's crossbelt thus occupied the left shoulder. The grey, loose-fitting trousers with zig-zag leather inserts and cuffs are typical field dress for Rifle officers of the period.

36. Maryland Rifle Volunteer, 1814
This was one of the more reliable American volunteer units of the war, which distinguished itself in the defence of Baltimore. Two riflemen, McComas and Wells, are believed to have killed the British Major-General Ross in this action, but as they were both killed themselves later in the battle their claim to

immortality as the avengers of the White House must remain uncertain.

The shako is the so-called Light Artillery style issued to artillery and rifle troops at this time; lacking the false front of the infantry shako, it tapers slightly from the top. Regular riflemen wore a round brass plate with a bugle-horn insignia and a green plume with the conventional cockade at the left side and yellow cords; this militiaman's green cords, white plume and central cockade are state distinctions. The hunting shirt or rifle frock had already passed into folklore, and was the normal summer field dress of regular and volunteer rifle units alike. Of green linen, with capes and fringes, it was usually decorated in yellow; again, the red fringes of the Maryland regiment were a state distinction, as was the red sash. The trousers are green, in the overall style. Equipment is simple and practical; each man carried his own long rifle, with a bullet pouch and a powder horn – these sophisticated weapons demanded more careful loading than pre-packed cartridges could provide, and the variety of bores in any unit with privately owned weapons would rule out any issue of mass-produced ammunition. Knives, hatchets, canteens and flasks of various types, and haversacks would all have been in evidence.

37. Sergeant, Battalion Company, British 93rd Regiment of Foot, 1815
The 2nd Battalion of the 93rd, Sutherland Highlanders, served in Newfoundland in 1814 and 1815. The 1st Battalion, some 900 officers and men, were shipped from England during 1814, arriving off Louisiana early in December. They went into action at the Battle of New Orleans on January 8th, 1815; by the end of the battle on the following day they had lost 75% of their strength. Apart from the Light Company, which was part of the successful assault on the American right flank, the unit was committed to the centre; American observers confirmed later that the giant Highlanders (picked for their height) stood like statues under a murderous fire of grape, roundshot and small arms fire, and died in their ranks.

This NCO wears the Hummel bonnet peculiar to the 93rd – it was more usually worn simply as a fatigue cap by Highland units, the Kilmarnock bonnet being worn in action. The red pompon on the bonnet identifies the battalion companies; grenadiers wore white, and the light company green. The normal infantry coatee has the lemon yellow facings of the 93rd,

and this shade also appears as a ground for the white rank chevrons. Two types of trousers were worn in this action; some troops still wore the usual grey fatigue trousers of the British infantry as a whole, while others had been issued with 'trews' in Government sett tartan. Short black half-gaiters were worn by all enlisted men.

Officers and sergeants of battalion companies wore the basket-hilted broadsword, popularly known as the claymore, and sergeants of battalion companies also carried the half-pike. To accommodate the sword on the left hip the wooden canteen of the usual British pattern, and the coarse canvas haversack, are slung on the right hip. Another indication of rank is the crimson sash, with a central stripe in the regimental facing colour, worn over the left shoulder by Highland units.

38. United States Infantryman, 1814
The clothing shortages which afflicted the US Army in this period resulted in many of the newly raised regular infantry regiments going into battle dressed in the grey kersey fatigue uniforms more properly worn only for working details. After the victory of the regular units at Chippewa in 1814, when men dressed in this fashion marched steadily into smashing British volleys and earned the highest compliment in the enemy commander's vocabulary – 'Those are regulars, by God!' – the grey uniform became a mark of pride. This soldier, his equipment bundled into a blanket roll in the absence of a haversack, wears the grey 'roundabout' jacket and loose trousers of the fatigue uniform; his shako is the only strictly regulation item in the whole outfit.

39. American General, 1814
This general officer wears the very smart and becoming uniform prescribed for generals and their staffs in 1813. The blue single-breasted coat is decorated with a herringbone pattern of black silk frogging on the chest, and has ten gold 'bullet' buttons, almost spherical in shape. The epaulettes are of heavy gold bullion, and the large *chapeau bras* is decorated with black silk ribbon and bullion tassels. The cockade has a gilt eagle badge in the centre. The high boots are of the pattern reserved for generals and staff officers only.

40. Private, British 21st Regiment of Foot, 1814-15

The 21st Regiment of Foot (Royal North British Fusiliers) saw extensive American service in several wars. In the summer of 1814 it formed part of Major-General Ross's force in the famous march on Washington, and entered the city first; it was men of the 21st who burned down the White House and the Capitol. The regiment saw little action for a while thereafter, withdrawing to Jamaica to reorganise; but in January 1815 it fought at New Orleans, losing more than half its strength.

This private wears the 1800 pattern 'stovepipe' shako, which was probably still in use by the 1st Battalion during the Washington expedition; the 1812 shako, with white cords, may have been issued during the unit's reorganisation in Jamaica. As a Royal regiment, the 21st wore the usual red jacket or coatee (bright red for officers and sergeants, and a coarser brick-red shade for other ranks) with blue facings. The shoulder wings of the enlisted men were replaced by bullion and scale metallic wings for officers. This soldier wears the usual grey coverall fatigue and field trousers, with half-gaiters and boots.

The full field equipment of the Napoleonic Wars is illustrated here. The white crossbelts support a socket bayonet on the left hip and a cartridge box behind the right hip. Other shoulder straps support the haversack and canteen on the left hip. White shoulder harness, with a narrow horizontal strap across the chest, supports the black canvas pack, with a rolled blanket strapped to the top. The smoothbore 'Brown Bess' musket is carried. Equipment carried by each man on the march would comprise sixty rounds of ball ammunition, spare shoes and clean shirts and stockings, and three days rations.

PLATE 6

26

29

27

28

30

55

PLATE 7

31

33

34

32

35

PLATE 8

36

39

37

38

40

4 Towards Professionalism

History repeated itself after the close of the War of 1812; despite the urging of officers and administrators of experience and vision, Congress determined to cut back the strength of the United States Army to a dangerously low figure. The army stood at 33,000 in 1815; Congress quickly cut it to 10,000, comprising eight regiments of infantry, one of horse artillery, and eight battalions of heavy artillery. The dragoons were once more disbanded; luckily various vital services and departments survived the axe, notably the General Staff, and departments of ordnance, medicine, finance and purchasing. The able and energetic John Calhoun fought to preserve the effectiveness, or at least the potential, of the peacetime forces during his term as Secretary of War. When Congress pressed one of their favourite measures – the cutting of the established strength to match actual strength – he tried to preserve the skeleton of all the units, ready for possible wartime expansion, but he failed. By 1821 Congress had cut the army to 6,000 officers and men in seven infantry and four artillery regiments, with companies of only 42 men. The previous organisation of the army into Northern and Southern commands, held by Generals Jacob Brown and Andrew Jackson, was changed to one based on Eastern and Western departments led by Winfield Scott and Edmund Gaines. Brown was brought to Washington as – in due course – Commanding General of the Army; Jackson retired to become Governor of Florida.

This whittling process was carried on against a background of sporadic Indian fighting. In 1817 raids by Seminoles from Florida on American territory and settlements in Georgia led to cautious orders from Washington for Jackson to cross the border but to respect Spanish posts – a sort of early 'hot pursuit' doctrine. The peppery Jackson

An Ogden plate showing enlisted men of foot (left) and mounted (right) branches in about 1855. The coloured cap band, coat collar, and cuffs have all given way to welts of coloured piping in the branch identification shade. The brass scale epaulettes are universal among non-commisioned ranks. Note the First Sergeant's sword, sash and crossbelt. *US National Archives*

61

The shell-jacket of the mounted troops, introduced during the 1830s when the Dragoons appeared once more on the roll of the Army. The worsted 'lace' on the collar and cuffs and around the front and bottom of the dark blue jacket was in the branch colour—yellow for the Dragoons, scarlet for the mounted artillery after about 1845. The star and bar insignia on the cuff is unexplained; it is thought to be a volunteer device of some sort, not a regular insignia. *Joseph Rosa*

promptly raised and led a force of some 1,500 local volunteers and the same number of Creek Indians on a three-month rampage through Spanish territory, which effectively stunned the Seminole but caused a diplomatic furor – the United States was in the process of negotiating with Spain for the peaceful transfer of Florida to the Union. After a ticklish round of conferences a compromise was reached; and two weeks after Jackson withdrew his troops Spain ceded Florida to America, in return for recognition of the Sabine River as the southern boundary of the Republic.

For the next twenty years the lines of tiny stockades and blockhouses manned by little groups of regulars inched westward across the map of the continent, spearheading the migration of the trappers, traders and farmers who pushed back the frontier. The troops, as much government sponsored explorers as soldiers, made many incredible journeys in totally unknown country. In 1833 the regular cavalry was resurrected once again, with the authorisation of a regiment of dragoons to escort the overland wagon trains now pushing through Oregon to California.

Of the many confrontations with Indians which took place in those years the two most important were Black Hawk's War and the Second Seminole War. Black Hawk, chief of the Sac and Fox, attempted to form a confederacy and drive the white man from the tribal lands in Illinois which he had appropriated. Failing to interest the British in Canada in underwriting this venture, Black Hawk crossed the Mississippi into Illionois at the head of his people, with a fighting strength of some 500 warriors. Brigadier-General Atkinson, commanding at Ft Leavenworth, Kansas, was ordered into the field with regular troops of the 6th Infantry and large numbers of Illinois militia, most of them mounted. Meanwhile Winfield Scott was ordered to march from the east with about 1,000 regular infantry and artillery. After an inconclusive brush with Black Hawk most of the volunteers discovered pressing reasons for returning home; this freedom to limit their service to short periods at their own discretion was always the greatest weakness of the volunteer system. With 500 regulars and a small force of the hardier militiamen, Atkinson pressed on; and on August 2nd 1832 he attacked the Indians on the Bad Axe River, and dispersed them. Some 150 warriors were killed and wounded, and Black Hawk was captured. Scott arrived on the scene five days later with the vanguard of his force, having covered the 1,800 miles from Virginia in only eighteen days; he had used water transport wherever possible.

In 1835 the Seminoles burst into flame once more, massacring two sizeable parties of regular and volunteer troops. General Gaines's Department of the West was threatened by trouble along the Texas border, so Winfield Scott was given command of the planned expedition. Ignoring this fact Gaines raised a largely militia force of 1,000 men, commandeered supplies that were being assembled for Scott, and sailed for Florida on his own initiative. Saved from disaster only by the timely arrival of some of Scott's units, he soon withdrew to New Orleans, declaring Florida pacified. For the next six years Generals Scott, Jesup, Zachary Taylor and Walker Armistead discovered how empty that claim was. It was a hideous war, fought out savagely in the twi-lit hell of the swamps; and it eventually degenerated into a straightforward war of extermination. By the time some 3,000 starving survivors of the Seminole nation were finally dragged out and shipped west, 5,000 regulars and upwards of 20,000 short-term volunteers had seen action in the treacherous jungles of Florida. Of these, nearly 1,500 died of wounds or disease. The Seminoles were never able to muster more than about 1,000 warriors.

In 1838 Congress, perturbed by the lack

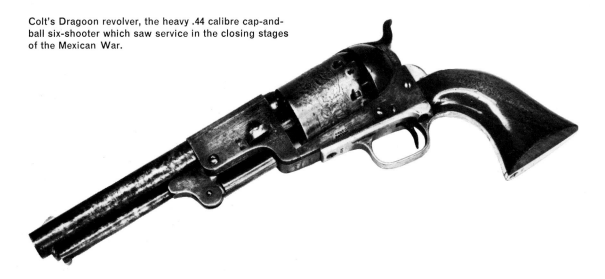

Colt's Dragoon revolver, the heavy .44 calibre cap-and-ball six-shooter which saw service in the closing stages of the Mexican War.

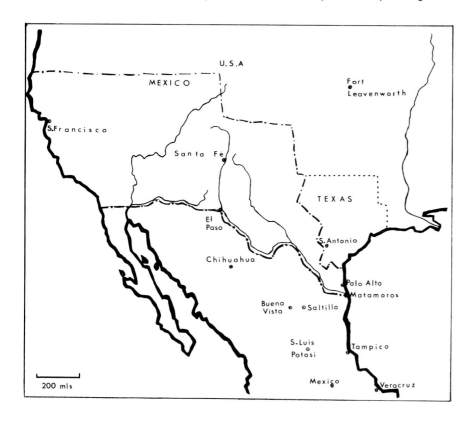

The Mexican War, 1846-48. The area within the broken-and-dotted lines was ceded to the United States by Mexico under the Treaty of Guadalupe Hidalgo.

of progress in Florida, authorised yet another expansion of the army. The establishment was raised to nearly 13,000 by increasing the sizes of existing units and raising a new infantry regiment. The numbers of units authorised were now eight regiments of infantry, four of artillery, two of dragoons, and the Corps of Engineers. (The second regiment of dragoons had been raised in 1836; it became a foot rifle unit in 1842, a Mounted Rifle regiment in 1844, and the 3rd Cavalry in 1861.) While the actual strength of most units was to remain at about 60% of establishment for many years, the principle of expanding or contracting units rather than raising and later disbanding them seems to have taken firmer hold in this period.

Trouble had been threatening along the southern frontier of the United States for many years, and in the 1830s and 1840s the uneasy relationship between a vigorous young America and an uncertain and newly independent Mexico was finally settled in blood. The present writer has no intention of even hinting at the progress of Mexican internal politics in this period, and will refer simply to 'Mexico', as meaning the current ruling faction at the time of the events described. His reasons may be deduced from the fact that between February 1836 and January 1848 Mexico was ruled – nominally – by twenty-three different governments, few of which gained or relinquished power peacefully. The longest term served by any one President of Mexico in this period was twenty-three months; the shortest, seven days. Santa Anna was President on no less than six separate occasions during this period.

Mexico had become independent in 1822-23, and had been recognised by the USA. Claiming the Sabine River as the national boundary and Texas – at this time largely uninhabited – as a province, Mexico pursued a liberal immigra-

Hall's 1843 percussion carbine, a rifled breechloader carried by the US Dragoons in the 1840s and 1850s. It is shown here with the ramp breech in the open position.

tion policy designed to attract settlers into Texas from the USA. By 1830 some 15,000 whites and many thousand Negro slaves had taken advantage of the invitation; but they never came to think of themselves as Mexicans, and chafed under a series of unstable regimes. Mexican policy changed radically, imposing hardship on those who had recently settled in Texas; open revolt flared up in 1835, and Texas declared itself an independent Republic in 1836. After the thirteen-day siege and eventual massacre of the Alamo garrison had fired the imagination of Americans, volunteers flooded south to swell Sam Houston's embryo Texan army; and American regulars were stationed south of the border at Nacogdoches for nearly six months, with a deliberately vague 'watching brief'. Sam Houston's 743 Texans decisively defeated Santa Anna's 1,600 Mexican regulars at San Jacinto on April 21st, 1836, and in March 1837 the USA recognized the Republic of Texas. Most Texans had looked no further than independence from Mexico, and confidently expected that the USA would quietly annexe Texas once the embarrassing necessity of actually fighting the Mexicans had been removed by the local forces. Unfortunately they had underestimated the diplomatic confusions of the day. The slavery question had become a furiously argued issue in the States, and the Texans were slave-owners of some determination. The two issues, slavery and annexation, became linked; and for nine years Texas

continued to exist as an independent state, ravaged by undeclared and savage guerilla warfare along the new border of the Rio Grande river. Mexico was determined to recover her lost province, and warned Washington that annexation would be considered an act of war.

In the end it was probably as much the commercial and economic potential of the little Republic as any moral question which decided the USA to risk war on the issue. The States voted in January 1845 on whether Texas should be invited to join the Union; the response was positive, and President James Polk offered Texas a place forthwith. The offer was accepted with alacrity, Mexico withdrew her diplomats from Washington late in March, and the United States were involved in their first major foreign war. It was to be a significant experience.

General Zachary Taylor led a force composed of the 3rd, 5th, 6th, 7th and 8th Infantry, two regiments of dragoons, and a mixture of artillery and horse artillery to Point Isabel, and built a fort on the Rio Grande opposite the Mexican town of Matamoros; and for two months the armies watched each other. Taylor's force was under strength in all units. It contained a high proportion of recent immigrants, and was officered by energetic but inexperienced young men. Few percussion weapons were available, and the bulk of the troops carried flintlocks.

65

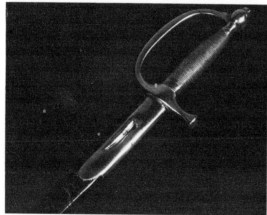

The 'eagle' shoulder-belt plate. *Hinton/Robson*

The Mexicans infiltrated over the river in increasing numbers, and patrol actions began to occur. Taylor withdrew the bulk of his men from their isolated forward position; and on May 3rd 1846 Mexican artillery began to shell the now lightly-held fort. A crossing in force soon followed, Taylor moved forward again to save the garrison, and the first battle of the war took place when the two armies collided at Palo Alto on May 8th. Outnumbered two to one, the American force won a splendid victory. The artillery proved particularly cool and reliable, and made a major contribution; and the 3rd and 5th Infantry formed squares and beat off the enemy cavalry in the finest Waterloo style. Taylor suffered only nine dead and forty-seven wounded, to the 700 Mexican casualties; unfortunately one of the nine was the dashing Major Ringgold, commander of the magnificent 'Flying Artillery'. The American force moved forward again the next day, fought a stiff action at the dry bed of the Resaca, and chased the Mexicans back over the Rio Grande. The lack of forage reported by forward patrols decided Taylor to stay where he was for the time being.

War was not officially declared until May 13th – one must bear in mind the distances and communication techniques of the day. Congress voted to double the strength of the army by increasing the infantry company to 100 men; added a regiment of Mounted Rifles to the establishment; and authorised the call-up of 50,000 volunteers for terms of not more than one year. President Polk envisaged a swift victory; Winfield Scott, Commanding General of the Army, knew better. Mexico had some 30,000 men under arms and a huge potential militia. The turbulent years since independence had ensured that the Mexican soldier was usually a veteran of at least one campaign; and the harsh and disease-ridden terrain promised to take a toll of the US forces. Eventually a three-pronged offensive was planned. Taylor should move westwards towards Chihuahua. Stephen Kearny, with a largely volunteer army assembled at Ft Leavenworth, would also move west and south, aiming for Santa Fé, and ultimately for California. The Navy was to blockade the east coast of Mexico, and to co-operate with Kearny in capturing the coastal areas of California.

The war did not turn out exactly as planned – which war ever has? – but the final outcome was an achievement of which America could be justly proud. Zachary Taylor's drive through northern Mexico saw the capture of Monterrey in September 1846, after house-to-house fighting of a very testing nature; Taylor's regulars stood up to it magnificently. Meanwhile Kearny took Santa Fé and plunged into the mountains heading for California; and another force under John Wool, some 2,000 strong, set out from San Antonio and struck south-westward for Parras, hoping to link up with Taylor in this rich and fertile area. By the beginning of December 1846 Taylor was in command of Saltillo and Victoria, Wool was at the gates of Parras, Kearny was in San Diego on the Californian coast, and naval landing parties had seized several ports and coastal areas.

While American forces now commanded large areas of northern Mexico, it was decided that to bring the war to a conclusion a new offensive must be mounted; an expedition should land at Vera Cruz and march inland to Mexico City. Winfield Scott was given command, and began to strip Taylor and other commanders of men to form the expedition. With 4,000 of his regulars and an equal number of volunteer units detached to Tampico for shipping to Vera Cruz, Taylor was soon left with only some 5,000 men in all, of whom only two dragoon squadrons and a small artillery unit were regulars. By February 1847 Taylor and Wool had pooled their slender resources, prudently but not in any immediate expectation of attack, and were occupying positions just south of Saltillo; it was the conventional wisdom that the main Mexican force would be committed at Vera Cruz, as security was non-existent and the coming campaign in the south was common knowledge. Unknown to Taylor the enemy leader Santa Anna had determined to take this opportunity of defeating the depleted American force in the north, and was marching from San Luis Potosi with some 15,000 men.

On February 21st American scouts reported the advance of the enemy, and Taylor immediately drew back to the more defensible Buena Vista area. The Mexican line of advance was up a narrow valley with high ground on each side; about 4,800 of the American troops, under Wool, were positioned on the shoulders of the hills, with a battery of artillery and a regiment of Indiana Volunteers at the head of the defile. Taylor himself was at Saltillo with some dragoons and the Mississippi Rifle Volunteers, commanded by Colonel Jefferson Davis. The battle opened on February 22nd and continued the next day; furious Mexican assaults were made in an attempt to dislodge the left flank and centre of the American position, and Santa Anna's troops gained considerable ground. Some American volunteers broke and ran, and the situation was critical when Taylor arrived in person with the Mississippi Rifles. Throwing this excellent volunteer unit, the artillery, and infantry from the less hazardous right flank into action on his weakened left, he saved the day. Hard fighting continued almost until sunset, but Santa Anna had lost nearly 2,000 casualties

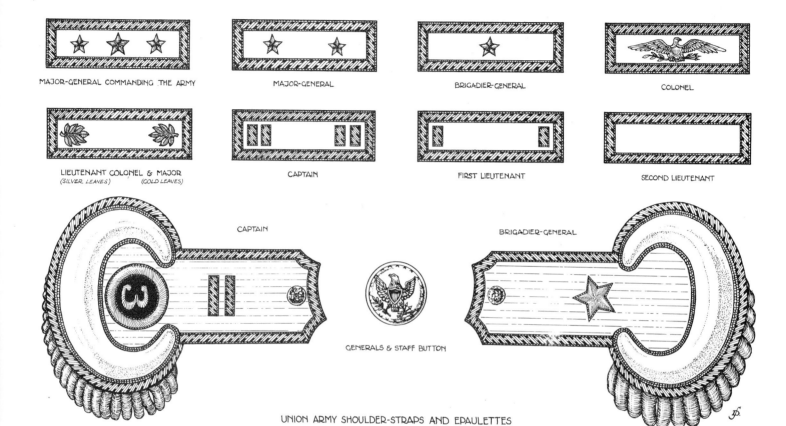

MAJOR-GENERAL COMMANDING THE ARMY

MAJOR-GENERAL

BRIGADIER-GENERAL

COLONEL

LIEUTENANT COLONEL & MAJOR
(SILVER LEAVES)   (GOLD LEAVES)

CAPTAIN

FIRST LIEUTENANT

SECOND LIEUTENANT

CAPTAIN

BRIGADIER-GENERAL

GENERALS & STAFF BUTTON

UNION ARMY SHOULDER-STRAPS AND EPAULETTES

Officers' shoulder insignia of the 1850s and 1860s; the 'boxes' worn on undress uniform at the time are still in use, on the US Army's latest full dress uniform. *David Scheinmann*

and had no more reserves; he withdrew his demoralised army, and in due time began a dispirited retreat to San Luis Potosi. Taylor had lost 265 killed, 450 wounded and a few missing, but he had won the hardest battle of the war.

About a week later a force of some 900 Missouri Volunteers under Colonel Doniphan, detached from Kearny's command and striking south from Santa Fé towards Chihuahua, met and defeated a much superior Mexican force at El Paso. This was the only other notable action in the northern zone of operations.

On the evening of March 9th 1847 the first men of Scott's expedition landed on a beach two miles south of Vera Cruz. This force comprised about 13,700 of whom some 5,700 were regulars; and Scott's staff included several young officers whose names, like that of the colonel of the Mississippi Rifles, would be heard again before many years had passed – Pierre Beauregard, George Meade, and Robert E. Lee among them. The landing was unopposed and went smoothly; the Mexican commander had only some 4,300 men, and in the face of such odds decided to keep them behind the city walls. A bombardment by sea and land forced the city to surrender without an assault, on March 27th. Scott advanced, and early in April ran up against a strong blocking position at Cerro Gordo, some thirty miles from Vera Cruz; Santa Anna, with an army of 12,000, was strongly entrenched in a pass in the mountains up which Scott must advance. The situation was almost a complete reversal of that at Buena Vista, but Santa Anna evidently had not learned from his mistakes. A reconnaissance led by the young Captain Robert E. Lee found a way around Santa Anna's left flank; Scott sent two of his three divisions round the Mexican position and cut its only road to safety while launching a volun-

teer division in a frontal assault. This was beaten off, but when the Mexicans found themselves surrounded they collapsed. For 431 American casualties Scott gained 3,000 prisoners, 4,000 muskets, and 43 cannon, and inflicted more than 1,000 casualties on the enemy.

An immediate advance along the remaining 170 miles of road between Cerro Gordo and Mexico City presented problems. Scott's force was being seriously reduced by disease, by difficulties of supply and communications, and by the departure of seven volunteer regiments whose term of service had now expired. Moving forward as far as Puebla, Scott bided his time while attempts to reach a negotiated peace failed – the failure following rapidly on Santa Anna's receipt of a 'down payment' of $10,000! Early in August, after rebuilding his force to a strength of some 10,000 men, Scott struck at the capital. He had no men to spare to guard his lines of communication back to Vera Cruz; in a step of great daring he deliberately abandoned his 'back door' and led his whole force up on to the plateau on which Mexico City stands.

The lakes and marshes which surrounded the city were traversed by causeways with strong defensive positions at the intersections, and commanded by several hills which were also fortified as screening positions before the city itself. One of these hills, the citadel of Chapultepec, had been chosen by Santa Anna as the main defensive system outside the city, although many of the other screening works were also garrisoned. Two brisk clashes on August 19th and 20th saw the Mexicans pushed out of most of these forward defenses, and a two-week lull then followed while the Mexicans held out the possibility of a negotiated peace. When it became clear that this was merely a time-wasting ruse, in the first week of September, the assault was resumed; and

The black Hardee hat, which appeared in the late 1850s as full dress wear in place of the *chasseur*-style cap. Only the mounted artillery retained a plumed shako for full dress. This Hardee hat displays the saxony-blue cords of the infantry; the company letter, regimental number and bugle-horn branch insignia, in brass; and the eagle pin which held up the brim. The black feather plume is just visible. *Katcher*

after bloody fighting Chapultepec fell on September 13th. It was the last major battle of the war; Santa Anna and the remnant of his force slipped out of the city during the following night, and the unlucky general abdicated the Presidency. His last troops were convincingly beaten shortly thereafter, in an attempt to capture an American supply train on the Vera Cruz road.

The present writer's purpose in describing the actual course of operations in greater detail in this chapter than in others is to demonstrate the very substantial improvement in the skill and professionalism displayed by the United States Army in the Mexican War. There were still areas of weakness, but the generally good performance of all arms in these campaigns served to throw a light on those weaknesses, identifying them and leading, eventually, to their elimination. This was a war the like of which the USA had never seen, and considering the scope of the problems faced by the armies of Taylor, Kearny, Wool and Scott, their success is doubly impressive. The regulars, noticeably more disciplined and steady than in earlier years, fought pitched battles of a conventional nature for the first time in thirty years, and acquitted themselves well against regular infantry, cavalry and artillery. They stormed defensive works of some strength and sophistication; captured a hostile city street by street; and marched thousands of miles through a harsh and unknown country completely different from the terrain they were accustomed to. They were shipped overseas and landed on an enemy beach in considerable strength. They shifted for themselves in countryside which did not offer plentiful pickings.

The supporting branches had, almost without exception, operated with an efficiency which could hardly have been expected in view of their difficulties. As in all 19th Century armies the losses from disease were appallingly high by modern standards, but they were no worse than any army of that time could have achieved. There were breakdowns of communications, failures of supply – but far fewer than might have been expected considering the length of the supply lines through a hostile wilderness. In the aftermath of the war the army was the only effective administration in Mexico, and records suggest that the unexpected and wholly unfamiliar task was carried out with reasonable justice and efficiency.

The Treaty of Guadelupe Hidalgo on February 2nd, 1848 gained for America a huge new tract of territory previously the property, in name at least, of Spain and Mexico; the new possessions encompassed what is now Arizona, New Mexico, Utah, Nevada, California, and parts of present-day Wyoming and Colorado. Emigrants and gold-hungry adventurers, traders and trappers, religious sectarians and farmers dreaming of the fertile acres to the west – in their thousands the new pioneers moved out into the unknown; and it was the army who had to guide them and guard them on their journey. Between 1848 and 1860 there were between twenty and thirty distinct 'wars' between white man and red; in 1857 alone the army mounted thirty-seven separate expeditions which involved an actual armed clash and the suffering of casualties, not to mention the many other missions which were uneventful. All patrolling and campaigning was carried out in country which if not actually harsh, was at least totally devoid of the immediate necessities beyond water and game; all other supplies had to accompany the columns, on wagons or mules or packhorses or the soldiers' backs.

It would serve no purpose – and would be impossible for reasons of space – to detail the many actions fought by the army during this period. Suffice it to say that the constant campaigns, and the splitting of the army into small units widely scattered over vast distances, fostered an excellent spirit of self-sufficiency and uncomplaining toughness among the regular regiments.

One campaign which deserves a few lines, if only for its novelty, is the expedition against the Mormons. The Church of Jesus Christ of Latter-Day Saints had set up their own communities in the Utah Territory, and in 1857 word came to Washington that they were defying Federal authority. What truth there was in these charges is still disputed, but it is beyond dispute that President Buchanan's despatch of 2,500 troops to escort the government commission of enquiry was an example of conspicuous 'overkill'. Alarmed, as well they might be, by the approach of the 5th and 10th Infantry, eight companies of the 2nd Dragoons and two batteries of artillery, the Mormons raided the column while it was still some distance from Salt Lake Valley, managed to separate the troops from the wagon train, burned the latter, and made off with many of the cavalry mounts. The discomfited expedition spent a hungry winter in the Rockies, until reinforced the next spring by another 3,000 men from all branches of the regular army. An agreement was reached with the resourceful Mormons before a bloodbath could ensue.

The internal tensions which had been building up in the Union for decades – tensions sparked by, but considerably more complex than, the slavery issue – came to a head in 1860 with the election to the Presidency of Abraham Lincoln. By February 1861 South Carolina, Georgia, Alabama, Florida, Mississippi, Louisiana and Texas had passed ordinances of secession, declaring themselves no longer within the Union, and taking possession of

Federal forts, arsenals and naval facilities. Eight further 'slave states' (Delaware, Maryland, Virginia, North Carolina, Kentucky, Tennessee, Missouri and Arkansas) remained in the Union but seethed with unrest. The only military posts still realistically controlled by the national government within the new Confederacy were Forts Sumter and Pickens, at Charleston Harbor and Pensacola on the Gulf coast of Florida, respectively. Southern-born officers began to resign their commissions in the regular forces. Jefferson Davis, veteran of the Black Hawk War and Mexico, was sitting as President of the Confederate States of America in Montgomery, Alabama. It was a powder-keg situation; Lincoln moved cautiously, determined not to take action which could precipitate the other slave states into seceding from the Union, and determined to maintain the foothold which the two forts represented. Hasty Confederate action forced his hand, however; on April 12th, 1861, after a demand that the commander surrender the fort to local forces had been rejected, Fort Sumter was bombarded by Confederate cannon and forced to capitulate. The incident polarised public opinion, and Lincoln called upon the governors of the loyal states to furnish volunteers to save the Union. Most of Virginia, North Carolina, Tennessee and Arkansas joined the Confederacy, and the War Between The States began.

PLATES 9,10,11

41. United States Infantryman, 1825
In the early 1820s the army's uniform became smarter, more standardised and more original with the appearance of several new items. This private in parade dress wears the bell-crowned shako introduced in 1821 for company officers and men of all branches. The white pompon indicates the infantry; the colours of other branches were yellow (artillery), white with red tops (light artillery), and yellow and green for light infantry companies and riflemen respectively. Between 1825 and some time in the 1830s each infantry regiment was required to include a company of light infantry or riflemen, and a grenadier company, in the fashion of some European armies; the plumes of the latter were red. The badge, an eagle grasping an olive branch and a sheaf of arrows, was in gilt or white metal according to the branch, as were the chin-scales; the cords, in worsted or bullion according to rank, also followed the branch colour, being either yellow or white, gold or silver.

The dark blue 1821 pattern full dress coatee has lace decoration on the collar in the branch colour, and shoulder wings in the same shade. Rank could no longer be indicated by epaulettes, and this period saw the introduction of reversed chevrons on the forearm, in the branch colour, for non-commissioned officers. The officer's pattern coatee had large metal and bullion fringed wings on the shoulders, gold or silver according to branch, and rank was therefore indicated by bullion chevrons reversed on the upper arm. The buttons of all ranks followed the branch identification sequence. Pipe-clayed crossbelts are still worn; it was to be ten years before the waistbelt appeared.

42. Second Lieutenant, 1st US Dragoons, 1835
The revival of the regular cavalry took place with the raising of the United States Regiment of Dragoons in 1833. Field and parade uniforms were authorised for these mounted troops; this troop officer wears the full dress version.

The shako, made of a black wool or felt material with patent leather top, band, peak and strap, bore a gilt star with a central silver eagle device for all ranks. The gilt metal plume-holder supports a white horsehair plume; slightly less elaborate plumes were worn by enlisted men, and plumes with an added strip of red hair by field officers. The cords and

elaborate tassels were of gilt bullion material for officers, of yellow worsted for enlisted men. Later the mounted artillery were issued with these shakos, with red distinctions replacing the dragoon yellow, and red plumes.

The dark blue double-breasted coatee has yellow distinctions on the collar, cuffs and tail turn-backs, but the two former areas are obscured by gold lace decoration. The exact rank is indicated by the two gold buttons and lace loops on the cuffs. The coatee worn by enlisted men had much less elaborate gold lacework on the collar, exposing the yellow cloth, and a pointed strip of lace around the edge of the yellow cuff; their epaulettes, unfringed for the junior non-commissioned officers and fringed with yellow worsted for the senior ranks, were of cloth rather than metallic thread. The blue-grey trousers of this officer are distinguished by a double yellow stripe. Other indications of commissioned rank are the red sash knotted on the right, and the gilt sword-knot on the sabre. He is examining the strangely shaped black leather forage cap worn in the field by men of both foot and mounted branches between 1833 and 1839; it was worn without insignia, and could be folded flat across the top for carrying and packing.

43. Corporal, Fusilier Company, 'Allende' Line Infantry Battalion; Mexican Army, Texas, 1836
A soldier typical of the army which Santa Anna led against the Alamo, this corporal of riflemen displays the confusions and shortcomings of the Mexican forces of that period. His uniform is a mixture of 1823, 1832 and 1833 regulations, and has suffered during the long march north through the deserts which Santa Anna's army had to complete before beginning operations.

At the time of the first serious clashes between Mexican troops and Texans in 1835 the army consisted of battalions and regiments which in fact could field only companies and squads; a complicated system of local recruitment and several classes of militia had fallen into complete confusion. The army which took the Alamo was composed of 6,000 raw conscripts, their units and uniforms organised on a strictly ad hoc basis; they had marched a thousand miles from San Luis Potosi in two months, marking the desert trails with their corpses and abandoned gear. By the end of 1835 the old units had been fused, nominally, into the Line Infantry Battalions Hidalgo, Allende,

Morelos, Guerrero, Aldama, Jimenez, Landero, Matamoros, Abasolo and Galeana, all named after War of Independence leaders. (Six cavalry regiments formed at the same time were named after battles of that war.)

The corporal wears the old pattern shako with brass plate and scales and a plume in the national colours, distinguished by the green cord and tassels of the riflemen. His 'Turkish blue' coat with red collar, cuffs, piping, turnbacks and epaulettes is from the batch ordered in 1833; it still retains the number of his old battalion on the collar. The diagonal stripe on the forearms is the rank insignia, retained from the 1823 regulations. The cuff patch is the mark of a 'Preference Company' – ie, riflemen and grenadiers. The white canvas trousers of the Mexican peasant were widely used; it may be imagined that the quartermaster service was not at a peak of efficiency. The weapon illustrated is the British Baker Rifle; this was sold in large numbers to Mexico, and the old 'Brown Bess' Tower pattern musket was the standard arm of the line companies. Equipment consists of a tin cartridge box and the Baker sword-bayonet slung on crossbelts; a wooden canteen; and a cow-hide pack with a blanket rolled and strapped to the top. The thin switch was a privilege of corporals only; used to urge on the troops to greater efforts, it is a hang-over from 18th Century Spanish colonial military regulations.

44. United States Army Ordnance Sergeant, 1840
The full dress uniform worn by this senior non-commissioned officer invites immediate comparison with that of the Dragoon officer in 42, and is very similar.

The shako is the infantry and artillery model of 1832, with artillery distinctions; the ordnance department had been merged with the artillery by Congressional order in 1821. It is of black 'beaver' with patent leather trim, tapering very slightly towards the top; the slightly dished peak of the enlisted men's version illustrated here was replaced by a flat peak on the officer's model. This soldier has gilt artillery insignia – crossed cannons – and national insignia, and a red plume in a gilt holder; infantry enlisted men would have worn a white metal bugle-horn in place of the cannon, a white metal eagle, and a white plume. The height of the plume varied, but is thought to have been twelve inches for sergeant-majors and similar grades (such as ordnance sergeant) and eight inches for sergeants and below. Officers wore falling plumes of cock-feathers in the appropriate colour.

The ordnance sergeant was a senior specialist on any post; one was assigned to every station and fort to supervise arms and ammunition. His rank is indicated by the four buttons and yellow cuff patches on the sleeves, the heavy fringed epaulettes of yellow worsted and brass, and the sash and sword. The plain collar of the coatee is trimmed with yellow, and the blue-grey trousers have a dark blue stripe, indicating the branch.

45. United States Infantryman, Mexico, 1846
The magnificent regular infantry soldier of the Mexican War, in his normal field dress. The US Army had worn a forage cap of old coat cloth as early as 1825; the tall shakos worn on parade were obviously impractical as working garb. The early type, of roughly the same shape as that illustrated, was replaced in 1833 by the folding leather type held by the officer in **42**; this, in turn, was replaced by the type illustrated here in 1839. Of dark blue wool with a black leather peak and strap, it has a flap at the back which can be lowered to protect the neck in bad weather. Bands coloured in the branch colours – white for infantry, yellow for dragoons, red for artillery – were sometimes worn, but by no means invariably. Similarly, company letters were sometimes pinned to the front of the caps.

The short pale blue fatigue jacket trimmed with white tape and piping had been undress wear in the regular infantry for twenty years or so; it was the universal field dress of the regulars in Mexico, although volunteer regiments wore considerably·more motley costumes. The crossbelt and waistbelt are white, with oval brass plates; they support the cartridge box, and the bayonet scabbard in a sliding frog – the infantry were still armed with flintlocks and socket bayonets. A cotton haversack is slung on the left hip, and the canteen is carried over it on a separate strap, often with a panikin ready to hand. On the march the pack and blanket roll would be hung about with useful extras – kindling wood, bags of grain, rice or beans, or a chicken 'liberated' from some village.

46. Second Lieutenant of US Infantry, Mexico, 1846
In the field United States regular officers in Mexico almost invariably wore the dark blue frock coat, with rank 'boxes' on the shoulders in

the appropriate colour of metallic braid. This officer has the silver insignia of the infantry; the lack of rank bars inside the 'boxes' identifies him as a Second Lieutenant. His buttons are also in infantry silver, and there is a white stripe down the out-seam of his pale blue trousers. The forage cap is of rather superior cut and material to that of the enlisted men, and has no rear flap. The sword slung on a single white crossbelt, and the red sash, are further distinctions of commissioned rank. A haversack and canteen are carried, and the remainder of the officer's effects are simply bundled into a blanket roll.

47. Trooper, United States Dragoons, Mexico, 1847
With the exception of the 1839 forage cap, worn here with a yellow dragoon band, this trooper wears the field uniform issued to the regular cavalry since their reappearance in 1833. The short dark blue jacket is piped, and decorated on the high collar, with yellow; in Mexico the mounted artillery and mounted riflemen wore the same uniform with red and black-and-gold distinctions replacing the yellow of the dragoons. The pale blue-grey trousers were distinguished, in the case of NCOs, by a stripe in the branch colour. The waistbelt is supported by a narrow shoulder belt, and the sabre scabbard could be hooked up to the belt for ease of movement. A sling with a snap-hook carried the flintlock carbine, and in the field a coarse linen or cotton haversack was worn on the left hip. Carbine ammunition was carried in a black cartridge box worn centrally on the back of the waistbelt.

In the years between the Mexican and Civil Wars, when the dragoons were scattered widely along America's remote frontiers, this uniform was frequently modified to personal taste. Leather 'breed' leggings, colourful bandanas, long hair and flowing moustachios, even ear-rings – all could be seen in the ranks of the dragoons at this time. On a more official note, company letters would normally be pinned to the cap band.

48. Texas Ranger, Mexico, 1847
The Texas Rangers had their origin as a force of irregular mounted constabulary during the revolution against Mexico. Texas not unnaturally provided volunteers for the Mexican War, and much of the forward scouting for the armies of Zachary Taylor and Winfield Scott was performed by Colonel Jack Hays' regiment of

Texas Rangers. They were of an appearance which frankly scandalised the regulars, but no doubt they terrified the Mexicans even more. They wore no military uniform or device of any description. Some wore buckskin, as illustrated here, and others every possible cut and shade of civilian shirt, jacket or coat. Wide slouch hats of various types, or wide-brimmed straws, were the order of the day. 'Mule-ear' boots or 'breed' leggings were popular, usually with huge spurs. Arms consisted of privately owned flintlock rifles, huge Bowie knives, the occasional captured Mexican sabre, lariats, and, invariably, a terrifying array of pistols. Initially these were the single-shot percussion type, but in 1847 a shipment of Colt's new six-shot percussion revolvers came up from Vera Cruz and the Rangers are reported to have added a brace of these each to their older artillery. Full beards and long hair are mentioned in reports of the time as being the normal fashion among Rangers. This formidable rider is examining the cap of a Mexican Jalisco Lancer.

49. Rifleman, First Mississippi Regiment (Rifle Volunteers), Mexico, 1847
This unit saved the honour of the American volunteers at Buena Vista by obeying the order to 'Stand fast!' of their wounded Colonel Jefferson Davis; indeed, at one point in the battle they charged Mexican cavalry on foot! Largely composed of well-born young Southerners and accompanied by a group of Negro slaves and body servants, the regiment was superior to most in its weapon – the new 1841 government pattern percussion rifle, obtained for them by Davis. The neat, simple and practical uniform is shown here – a red flannel shirt of military cut, a wide-brimmed straw hat, and white duck trousers. Government pattern cartridge boxes were carried on a white crossbelt, but no bayonets were issued and most volunteers carried the murderous Bowie or Arkansas knives instead.

50. Grenadier, Batallon Activo de San Blas; Mexican National Guard, Chapultepec, 1847
During the constant internal warfare which tore Mexico in the years prior to the Mexican-American War the armed forces underwent constant reorganisations, redesignations and amalgamations. Regular units were wiped out and rebuilt from Active Militia units, local conscripts, and the survivors of other units. Names and numbers disappeared, were resurrected, and disappeared once more, and

any attempt to trace a direct lineage between units of the 1835-37 period and units of the Mexican-American War would be tedious and time-consuming. A glance at surviving uniform regulations reveals an equally complex picture. Orders were issued, revoked, revived and abandoned in quick succession, and the chaotic supply and procurement situation made many of them meaningless in practical terms.

The grenadier illustrated is drawn from a Mexican source, and is believed to be an accurate representation of the dress worn by this battalion at the Battle of Chapultepec on September 13th, 1847. The 'Active Coast Guard Battalion of San Blas' was wiped out almost to a man on Chapultepec Hill, earning the admiration of American observers for its heroic defiance. This militia unit had a long and chequered history, beginning with its organisation as a local guard force for the area around the port of San Blas in 1824. For the next twenty years it marched all over Mexico under the flags of numerous and sometimes short-lived factional leaders, seeing much active service and heavy losses. In July 1845 it was at San Luis Potosi as part of the reserves for the planned reconquest of Texas, but it got involved in another revolution later that year and was marched to Mexico City by yet another rebel general. It remained in the capital until July 1846, being renamed as the 3rd Regular Infantry during this period. In September 1846 the renamed unit fought at Monterrey, in February 1847 at Angostura, and in April 1847 it was wiped out at Cerro Gordo. A new National Guard battalion in the process of formation at Guadalajara was given the honoured name of the old San Blas Battalion, and it was this reborn unit which was wiped out on Chapultepec Hill.

The grenadier wears the type of shako generally issued to National Guard units; there were more than twenty different types of military headgear currently in use in the army as a whole, and it is doubtful that the entire unit would have the same pattern. It is decorated with top and bottom bands of yellow metal, yellow metal chin scales, and an oval plate bearing the name of the battalion. The national cockade in green, white and red is surmounted by a round red pompon, identifying a grenadier company. The fringed red epaulettes are also an indication of grenadier status, as are the 'Preference Company' patches on the cuff. The grey frock coat piped in red was standard National Guard issue, and it is only the collar device – *BSB* for *Batallon San Blas* – which

identifies the unit. The red-piped blue trousers, white gaiters and black boots were worn by both National Guard and Line infantry. All buttons are in the yellow metal universally worn by Mexican infantry; both black and white crossbelts were common in 1847, but the type illustrated are taken from a Mexican painting of this unit. The weapon is the old 'Brown Bess' musket, a relic of Britain's wars with Napoleon which was sold off in vast numbers to customers such as Mexico by a canny government.

51. United States Dragoon, 1852

The Mexican and Seminole campaigns, and the sporadic frontier fighting which followed them, led to a realisation that widespread uniform changes were needed. The distinction between parade dress and fatigue and fighting dress was recognised, and the branch insignia of the whole army were standardised. The 1851 uniform regulations, which with later amendments are illustrated by the figures on this plate, covered a wide range of items.

This dragoon's most immediately noticeable feature is the change of branch colour from yellow to orange. The short cavalry soldier's jacket is identical in cut to that worn by the dragoons in Mexico, but all yellow distinctions have been replaced by the new shade. New epaulettes for all non-commissioned ranks of the dragoons and light (mounted) artillery are shown here, a scaled yellow metal design introduced in 1851. Above the cuffs appear new service stripes – 'hash marks' – in the branch colour, indicating two enlistments. A rectangular brass buckle bearing the national eagle motif within a wreath and against clouds, rays and stars fastens the black sword belt; the belt and buckle were authorised in 1851 for all ranks and branches.

The dragoon wears the new 'gig' cap which from 1851 to 1854 was worn by all branches, in place of the two types of shako illustrated in **42** and **44** on Plate 9. Of dark blue cloth with a black leather peak and strap, the cap has a broad band of material in the branch colour; a yellow metal company letter is fixed centrally to this band. A pompon in the branch colour rises from a ring at the top of a yellow metal plate bearing the national insignia. The bands and pompons of infantry, artillery and riflemen were in Saxony blue, scarlet and emerald green respectively, all with company or battery letters.

52. Captain of United States Riflemen, 1852

The 1851 reforms brought in the frock coat as

the normal dress of officers and enlisted men of the foot branches. The officer's pattern is shown here, a plain dark blue coat with a high collar and gold buttons down the front and at the wrist. Officers wore no collar ornaments. The full dress epaulettes of bullion cord were now charged with exact rank and unit insignia; this officer has the two silver bars of a captain embroidered on the strap, and a lozenge in the crescent which identifies his unit. This is in the form of a circle of emerald green cloth (signifying the Rifles) outlined in silver and bearing the gold '1' of the 1st Regiment of Riflemen. Infantry officers wore blue lozenges, artillery scarlet, and so forth. Rank insignia were worn in the sequence of Second Lieutenant (no insignia), First Lieutenant (one silver bar), Captain (two silver bars), Major (no insignia), Lieutenant Colonel (silver leaf), and Colonel (silver national eagle motif); Brigadier Generals, Major Generals and 'Generals in Chief' wore one, two and three large silver stars.

These full dress bullion epaulettes were interchangeable on the shoulders of the frock coat with rank 'boxes' for undress wear. These rectangles of gold braid enclosed patches of material in the branch colours, or dark blue for generals and staff officers, with the rank devices at both ends. Company officers' bars were in gold, and majors wore a gold leaf; from lieutenant colonels up the devices were in silver.

The branch colour was repeated in a narrow welt down the outer seam of the dark blue trousers; staff officers wore buff welts, recalling the buff of generals' trousers as far back as the Revolutionary War. The officer illustrated is adjusting the sword worn by all officers of foot branches, the black leather scabbard furnished with gilt metal. A more elaborate sword with a bronzed or browned steel scabbard was worn by generals and staff officers, and field and staff officers of regiments.

The officers' version of the 1851 'gig' cap bore no coloured band; the branch was indicated by a coloured pompon in the same way as the enlisted man's pattern, and branch and unit insignia were worn centrally on the front beneath the plate. The captain illustrated here has the gold vertical trumpet, with the silver regimental number in the loop, of the Rifles. Infantry officers wore a gold bugle-horn with a silver number in the loop; dragoons and artillery officers wore crossed sabres or cannons in gold, beneath a silver regimental number. Officers of corps and departments wore appropriate insignia in this position: a silver

'US' cypher in a gold wreathe for generals, staff officers, medical, pay, subsistence, and Judge Advocate's officers; a triple castle in silver within a gold wreathe for engineer officers; a gold bursting shell for ordnance officers, and so forth.

53. Private, United States Engineers, 1852
The enlisted men of the early 1850s wore a frock coat with nine buttons of very similar cut to that worn by officers. The engineer illustrated here, trying on his coat after alteration, perhaps, displays the distinctions of his corps. The 1851 regulations called for the pointed cuffs and high collar of the enlisted man's coat to be in the colour of his branch. The engineer and ordnance branches, however, wore plain dark blue collars and cuffs with piping around the edges in yellow and crimson respectively. Similarly the 'gig' caps of these branches had plain dark blue bands with coloured piping along top and bottom edges; and instead of unit letters or numbers, these branches wore their corps badges on cap and collar – a triple-towered castle for the engineers and a bursting shell for the ordnance, both in yellow metal. The cap pompons of engineers and ordnance were black-over-buff and crimson-over-buff respectively; other specialist troops wore light blue-over-buff (quartermaster branch), emerald green-over-buff (medical personnel), royal blue-over-buff (subsistence department), and so forth.

From 1854 the coloured band worn on the cap by the main branches of the army was discontinued in favour of a line of piping in the branch colour following the top edge of the band, and from this time on the lower welt disappeared from the caps of engineers and ordnance personnel. The reason for this step is thought to have been the discovery that the materials used for these coloured distinctions were subject to rapid and uneven fading, giving a most unsoldierly appearance on parade!

54. Corporal, United States Infantry, 1858
The full dress of the infantryman in the years immediately preceding the Civil War.

The coloured collars and cuffs of the 1851 regulations have now completely given way to dark blue outlined in piping of the branch colour, presumably for the same reason as the abandonment of coloured cap bands. The regimental numbers worn on each side of the collar by troops of the main combat branches

also disappeared in 1858, as did the worsted fringed epaulettes in the branch colour worn on the frock coat for parade occasions since 1851. All branches now wear a metallic scaled epaulette in brass, very similar to that worn by the mounted troops since 1851. The rank chevrons authorised in 1851, in the branch colours, are retained. The 'gig' cap has been replaced as full dress wear for both foot and horse by the Hardee hat, a wide-brimmed high-crowned black felt normally worn with the brim pinned up on the left. The pin is very similar in design to the eagle plate worn on the 'gig' cap. The bugle-horn branch insignia of the infantry, and the company letter, are retained, and the hat is further distinguished by cords in the branch colour and a black feather plume. The cartridge box for the percussion Springfield rifle is worn behind the right hip slung on a black crossbelt, and the waist belt supports the bayonet and the small pouch for percussion caps.

55. Fatigue dress, 1858
The working dress of the American regular of the late 1850s was the simple 'sack' coat and the well-known 'bummer's cap'; for fatigues these would be worn unadorned, for other duties rank chevrons and leather gear might be added. Initially this dress was issued simply to save the frock coats and rather elaborate headgear from damage during heavy work, for which they were obviously unsuitable. Within a few years, as the universal fighting uniform of the Federal soldier, this rig would acquire fame and dignity.

PLATE 9

41

44

42

43

45

PLATE 10

46

49

47

48

50

PLATE 11

51

53

54

52

55

5 Blue and Butternut

Europeans frequently fail to grasp the sheer impact on the national life of the United States, then and since, of the Civil War of 1861-65. The English Civil War of the 1640s was enormously significant in the evolution of our society, and involved the clash of fundamental principles; but it is comfortably cushioned by more than three hundred years of elapsed time, and even in contemporary terms its impact on the day to day life of the population was less than we probably imagine. In the case of the war between the States, the bald statistics go a long way to explain why the echoes of civil war are still to be heard in America after more than a century.

The total population of whites and Negros at that time is estimated at some $32\frac{1}{2}$ million souls. When the nation divided, some $22\frac{1}{2}$ million supported the Union cause, and rather more than nine million the Confederacy. The Union put some 2,200,000 men into uniform during the whole course of the war, the Confederacy just over one million – roughly one in eleven, and one in nine, of their total populations of all ages, all races and both sexes. Of those who wore Union blue, it is known that some 100,000 were sixteen years of age, and another 100,000 were fifteen; in other words, of every eleven Union soldiers, one was sixteen *or less*. Soldiers of ten years of age have been reliably recorded. No comparable figures are available for the Confederacy, but they would certainly equal those of the Union. The peak strengths of the two sides in terms of men in uniform at any one time (1864-65) were approximately 1,045,000 and 485,000, Union and Confederate respectively.

Comparison of these totals with the casualty figures produces some brutal human equations. Such records as survive are obviously not completely reliable, bearing in mind the conditions of the time; Confederate records, in

A most interesting print taken from a period tintype, showing an unidentified Negro corporal in a version of Union Army uniform. The coat is the full dress frock, piped in the branch colour, and worn here with the collar turned down in strictly non-regulation style. The *kepi* seems to have the waterproof cover in place. *Chicago Historical Society*

Typical company of Union infantry, photographed near Harper's Ferry. The fixed sword-bayonets identify the rifles as Springfield Model 1855 weapons. At the front of the company stand the drummer, the First Sergeant, and a company officer with drawn sword. *Radio Times Hulton Picture Library*

Overleaf (left)
Reproduction—a Union volunteer infantry private of 1864. He wears the typical fatigue and field uniform, with dark blue *kepi*, dark blue 'sack' coat and light blue trousers, all of heavy wool. The leather gear is black with yellow metal furniture. He holds the 1864 Springfield rifle-musket; a socket bayonet hangs from the left hip in a simple frog. A tin canteen covered in grey wool, and a black tarred canvas haversack, are slung to hang on his left hip. The 1864 knapsack, with rolled blanket strapped on top, is also of tarred canvas. *Katcher*

Overleaf (right)
Reproduction—a Union mounted artilleryman of c1863. He wears the short dark blue shell jacket trimmed with scarlet braid, a dark blue *kepi* and sky blue trousers heavily reinforced in the crutch. The sabre suspenders of the sword belt hang loose—most artillerymen left their sabres in the battery wagon—and this soldier's weapon is the 1851 Colt's Navy revolver, carried in the issue holster. The .36 calibre Navy Colt was used by all branches of both armies in the Civil War, although the official US sidearm was the heavier .44 Army model. *Katcher*

particular, are sketchy in certain areas. Nevertheless one may present the following figures with some confidence:

	USA	CSA
Died in battle or of wounds:	110,100	94,000
Died in prison camps:	30,200	26,000
Died of disease:	224,000	60,000
Died of other causes:	34,800	Unrecorded
Total deaths	399,100	180,000+?

Rounding off fractions, one may therefore conclude that of every eleven men who wore blue between 1861 and 1865, including non-combatants, and including more than 300 regiments which were never committed to battle, two men failed to return. Statistics also show that of the nine who did see their homes again, two were wounded. Of every five men who wore Confederate uniform, one failed to return and another was wounded. Of the combined uniformed strength of the nation, one man in five never came home and another was wounded. This figure of roughly 20 per cent deaths among those engaged should be compared with British losses in the First and Second World Wars – 13.9 per cent and 4.5 per cent respectively. The true impact of the American Civil War now begins to emerge.

It was a war which saw the first widespread use of a practicable machine gun and a repeating rifle. As always, the forcing house of war brought along advances in destructive technology; the land mine and the torpedo, the ironclad ship and the aerial observer all had their debut. The science of military entrenchments and field works moved forward enormously in those short years; so, it should be said, did the aid and care of the wounded. The widespread use of railways to further and support operations was another new feature

of this war, and communication moved firmly from the age of the mounted courier into the age of the telegraph.

The high incidence of casualties was reflected at unit level; in this war, just as on the battlefields of Europe fifty years before, whole regiments were layed low in their ranks. At the Battle of Antietam in September 1862 the 1st Texas Infantry suffered 82 per cent casualties without breaking. Examples of regiments remaining in the line after suffering more than 50 per cent casualties are too numerous to list. At Gettysburg in July 1863 the losses of some units almost stagger the imagination. In this single battle 40,300 men were killed or wounded; of the Union troops engaged, 21 per cent were casualties – on the Confederate side, 30 per cent. Of every three Confederate soldiers who went into the battle, one was hit. The 26th North Carolina Infantry went into battle with just over 800 men; by the

Contents of a typical Civil War soldier's haversack. Clockwise, from tarred canvas haversack at top centre: White cotton food bag, which buttoned inside haversack. Tintype of wife in gutta-percha frame. Onions, piece of hard-tack. 'Housewife', with needles, thread and buttons. Bible, and spectacles; this bible was found on the field of Gettysburg. Tin mug, straight razor and cardboard razor case. Pre-stamped envelope marked 'Soldier's Letter'. Fork, spoon, and paper and coin money. Copy of Harper's Weekly. War Department publication, *Rules for the Management of the model 1861 Rifle-musket.* Tin plate. In the left foreground are musket tools—combined nipple-wrench and screwdrivers, tumbler punches, worm, and sight-wrench. *Katcher*

87

end of the third day it had 98 effectives. The famous charge by the Confederate General Pickett's Division on July 3rd included General Garnett's Virginia Brigade. The brigade charged 1,427 strong; 486 men returned to Seminary Ridge on their feet.

That the war could have continued for so long when the South was outnumbered so heavily and starved of almost every military necessity – except willpower and courage – was due in no small measure to the quality of the Confederate leaders. Jefferson Davis had commanded troops in battle in the Mexican War, and had since filled the posts of Secretary of War and Chairman of the Senate Military Affairs Committee. Robert E. Lee is of course one of the outstanding figures of American military history, as deeply respected, if not as well loved, by the Union as by the Confederacy. Both he and General Beauregard had been Superintendents of West Point in their time. A quarter of the West Point graduates who fought in the war served in grey uniforms; a third of all the officers in the American army in 1861 joined the Confederacy. Many rose to major commands at remarkable ages, and it was not uncommon for brigades to be commanded by generals in their late twenties. The gay and brilliant 'Jeb' Stuart, commander of Lee's magnificent cavalry, was a Brigadier-General at the age of twenty-nine.

The cruel divisions of the Civil War extended through every level of life, and particularly in the professional military establishment. This relatively small and tight-knit club was split from top to bottom by conflicting loyalties. It should be remembered that when the war broke out the US Army had little over 1,000 officers. Every man knew, or had heard of, all his contemporaries. Confederate commanders found themselves facing old classmates, former commanding officers, cousins, brothers-

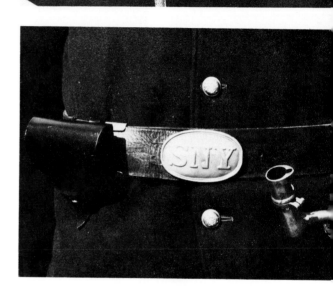

1861 US Army eagle belt-plate, and pouch for percussion caps. *Katcher*

Union volunteers often wore items marked with State insignia, such as this 'State of New York' belt-plate; note also the cap-pouch and bayonet frog. Rebel wits apparently translated the belt-plate insignia as standing for 'Snotty-Nosed Yank'. *Katcher*

Confederate States of America belt-plate, in this case marked on the reverse by its owner, who served with the 8th Texas. *Hinton/Robson*

in-law. Union officers faced their old instructors, the men who had recommended their promotions, and men who had drunk and joked with them at Washington balls and parties. Abraham Lincoln had four brothers-in-law in the Confederate Army. He had been personally responsible for the appointment to the Military Academy of the man who would become General George Pickett.

The cannon fire over Charleston Harbor on April 12th, 1861 ushered in a war for which, inevitably, nobody was ready. The small army (about 16,000 men) available to Lincoln was spread throughout the country in many detachments; and it should be remembered that while the struggle between 'Billy Yank' and 'Johnny Reb' was being fought out, other troops still had to guard the frontier against the Indian tribes – who took no little advantage of the white man's distraction. 'Kit' Carson, the legendary frontiersman, held a colonel's commission and command of the 1st New Mexico Volunteers during the war, and operated exclusively against the frontier Indians.

The skeleton of the professional army was fleshed out, on both sides, by the expedient of mobilising the various state volunteer regiments. This led to the appearance in the firing lines of many strange and colourful uniforms, reflecting the independence of these state units in the pre-war years, and the slightly carnival atmosphere which attended their functions. These regiments were partly social clubs for the local gentry, officered by the local hierarchy and often uniformed in some flashy and outlandish manner copied from current European fashions – thus the many regiments modelled on the French *Zouaves*. Although the regulars tended to sneer, and although it is true that many of these outfits found the actual experience of battle too much for their romantic illusions, it is not accurate

Reproduction—a Confederate infantry corporal of 1863. A plain black slouch hat is worn in preference to the regulation *kepi*. A grey shell jacket with sky-blue chevrons on each arm is fastened with Union infantry officer's buttons—a feature of several surviving rebel coats. The black belt, with cap-pouch and bayonet, is fastened with a plain oval brass plate. The shoes are civilian. The white duck haversack with bone buttons, and the blanket roll, are both original contemporary items. The wooden canteen is iron-bound, and has a linen strap. The weapon is the .54 calibre Austrian rifle-musket of 1853; the Confederacy imported about 27,000 of these, and at least one regiment of the Stonewall Brigade was armed with them. *Katcher*

An original Confederate artillery *kepi*, with a blue band and a red crown. *Hinton/Robson*

A common Confederate belt style, with a plain square frame buckle, and a Confederate-manufactured cap-pouch. *Katcher*

finery of the Volunteers was rarely seen on the actual battlefield after the first few campaigns. It was generally reserved for parade wear, and the standard issue blue uniform might be distinguished by some style of frogging or similar mark of origin. While the Northern troops moved towards uniformity of appearance, the Southern soldier, bedevilled by shortages and empty war chests, became more and more ragged. The smart grey gave way to homespun dyed with butternut to a neutral fawn shade – in many cases to frankly civilian dress with few, if any, military distinctions. Equipment was cut to the necessary minimum and rolled in a proofed 'gum blanket' around the body. While both sides practised considerable variation in the style of wearing clothes and equipment, it was the Confederate who generally came to resemble a farmer rather than a soldier. The soldierly qualities of the Confederate in battle are, however, beyond any faintest doubt.

The great strength of the Confederacy lay in its horsemen. Raised from a rural population who were used to horses from childhood, and containing no small number of wild and courageous cavaliers, the Southern regiments led with such conspicuous success by men like 'Jeb' Stewart and Nathan Forrest were frankly scornful of the Yankee cavalry blundering after them. Not until the great clash of sabres at Brandy Station in June 1863 did the Northern cavalry, shaped and polished by Buford and Sheridan, gain the confidence which was to remain their strength for years to come. One early move toward a more professional cavalry arm was the abandonment, after the First Battle of Bull Run in the summer of 1861, of the distinctions between Dragoons, Cavalry and Mounted Rifles.

The basic tactical formation of the Civil War was the regiment, nominally of ten companies

to regard them as ridiculous. They provided a corps of experienced drill-masters to lick into shape the thousands of volunteers flocking to the colours; and in some cases their record in battle was as proud as that of any regular regiment.

The dress of the Northern soldier became more uniform as the war progressed. With the strength of the nation's industrial areas behind them, the Northern regiments soon 'looked like an army' in their uniform blue. The gaudy

Famous view of General Philip Sheridan and other Union generals of the Army of the Potomac in 1874. Note the variety of dress it reveals; visible are both regulation frock coats, and civilian velvet-collared frocks with rank boxes added to the shoulders. The huge, soft-leather boots are typical, as is the dandyish style affected by the officer standing on the right; he wears a fancy shirt with a braided collar, and carefully arranged buttons. *Radio Times Hulton Picture Library*

Two types of Civil War canteen in close-up; tin covered with grey wool, and wooden bound with iron. The tin variety was often converted into a pair of plates by dropping it into the coals of a campfire, and springing the seam. *Katcher*

and totalling thirty officers and 1,300 men (in the Union armies). 'Nominally' is the key word; disease, and the many non-combatant details which the regiment had to provide from its own strength usually reduced this to an effective figure of some 800 rifles before battle was joined. Average regimental strengths in most campaigns were around the 500 level. Confederate strengths tended to be lower still, and by the beginning of 1864 companies with only thirty or forty effectives were not uncommon. In both armies the last year of the war saw frantic efforts to keep the ranks filled, by persuading volunteers on fixed terms to re-

The 1851 Colt's Navy revolver: a pistol cartridge box, in which packets of combustible cartridges were carried: and the hilt of an 1860 Light Cavalry sabre. *Stephen Russell/David Scheinmann*

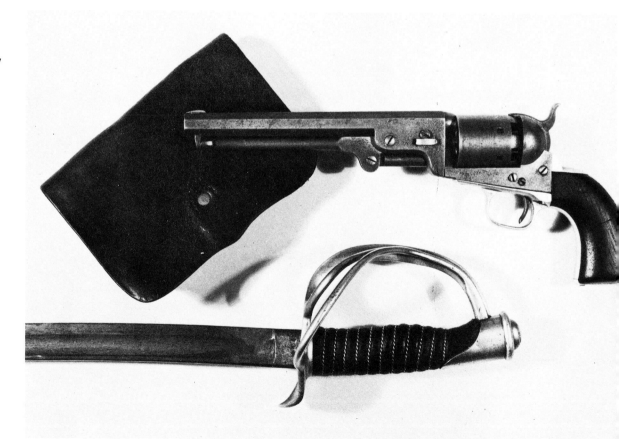

enlist for a bounty and generous leave, and by straightforward conscription.

For tactical purposes regiments were gathered in brigades, usually known by the name of the commanding Brigadier-General, consisting of anything between two and five regiments. The brigades were grouped in divisions, again, often known by the name of the commander. The divisions were grouped in corps, usually distinguished by a Roman numeral. An interesting feature of the Civil War was the adoption, widespread in the Union army, of simple divisional and corps insignia. This practice originated in an order by General Phil Kearney in June 1862, to the effect that men of his 3rd Division, III Corps should wear a piece of scarlet cloth. '. . . By the middle of 1863 most of the elements of the Army of the Potomac had adopted some sort of device. The basic design was that of the corps, while its colour usually represented a specific division within the corps.' (*Todd, op.cit.*). These simple cloth patches took the form of circles, squares, crosses, acorns, stars and similar designs, usually sewn to the top of the 'bummer's caps' or the front of slouch hats. Examples are illustrated in the plates.

While the early rush of volunteers to both flags often took the form of locally raised companies from some particular town or county, this regional independence soon disappeared, and with it some splendidly fanciful titles – Todd quotes that the 'Tyranny Unmasked Artillery' became Company K, 47th Virginia. The regiments retained their state identity, however. It was not usual for an entire brigade to be made up of regiments from the same state, but it did happen in a few cases, notably that of the Vermont Brigade; and it was not uncommon for brigades to contain regiments from the same general area, say three from one state and two from a neigh-

This print from an original contemporary ferrotype shows J. L. Baldwin, First Sergeant of Company G, United States 56th Colored Infantry. Note the piping at collar and cuffs—the jacket is made from a cut-down full dress frock coat. *Chicago Historical Society*

bouring state. The organisation of brigades seldom remained the same throughout the war, regiments being transferred from one duty to another according to strength and fitness, or local requirements.

Some brigades earned a name for themselves as brigades – that is, they forged an identity as units which 'stuck', overshadowing the identity of the individual regiments. Examples include the 'Iron Brigade' – also widely known as the 'Black Hat' Brigade from their habit of wearing the wide-brimmed full dress black Hardee hat in the field in preference to the low blue *kepi* or 'bummer's cap'. The Hardee hats were often replaced, in time, by ordinary civilian-purchase black slouch hats. The Iron Brigade was drawn from Western states, and for most of its active career comprised the 2nd, 6th and 7th Wisconsin Infantry, the 19th Indiana and the 24th Michigan. The brigade suffered the heaviest losses in proportion to its strength of any brigade in the Union army. (The heaviest outright loss of life was suffered by the Vermont Brigade.) A Confederate

formation which made a particular name for itself was the 1st Virginia Brigade, made up of the 2nd, 4th, 5th, 27th and 33rd Virginia Infantry and the Rockbridge Artillery – the latter unit hailing from a county of that name in the Shenandoah Valley. The brigade was commanded by Thomas Jonathan Jackson, and later took his immortal nickname for its own – 'The Stonewall Brigade'.

It was a particularly noticeable feature of Confederate regiments that the local connections retained their strength and meaning throughout the war. There were regiments in which ten or twenty members of the same local family might serve together. The officers were often local notables, the rural 'squires', known personally to the bulk of their men and with a tradition of taking the lead in all local affairs. This social structure gave the grey regiments the same high morale and unthinking loyalty which were a feature of British regiments with strong traditional local identities in the 19th Century. Other forms of special identity may be noticed. The 'Stonewall Brigade' pro-

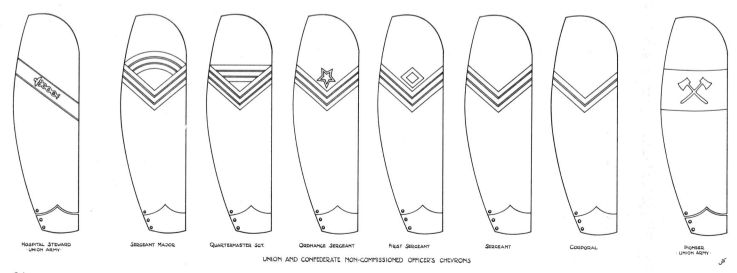

HOSPITAL STEWARD ·UNION ARMY·   SERGEANT MAJOR   QUARTERMASTER SGT.   ORDNANCE SERGEANT   FIRST SERGEANT   SERGEANT   CORPORAL   PIONEER ·UNION ARMY·

UNION AND CONFEDERATE NON-COMMISSIONED OFFICER'S CHEVRONS

vides two examples – the Rockbridge Artillery and the 'Liberty Hall Volunteers' of the 4th Virginia Infantry. The former became so popular that its recruitment had to be restricted by order of the brigade commander. It was largely manned by college graduates, with a high proportion of theological students, and its first commander was the rector of an Episcopal Church in Lexington; its four guns were named Matthew, Mark, Luke and John. The 'Liberty Hall Volunteers' were a rifle company in the 4th Virginia, of which 57 of the

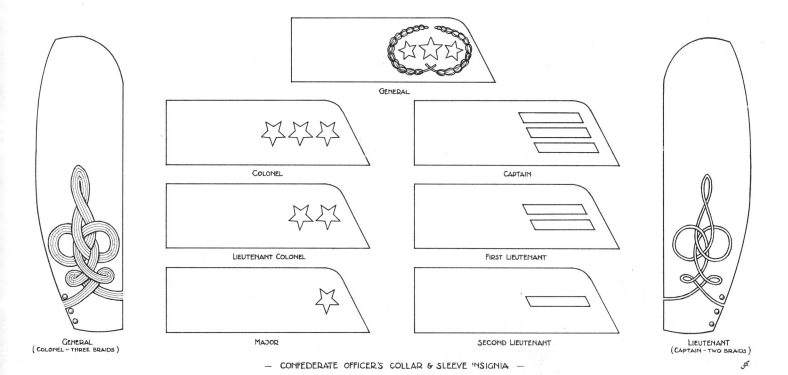

GENERAL

COLONEL

LIEUTENANT COLONEL

MAJOR

CAPTAIN

FIRST LIEUTENANT

SECOND LIEUTENANT

GENERAL
(COLONEL – THREE BRAIDS)

LIEUTENANT
(CAPTAIN – TWO BRAIDS)

— CONFEDERATE OFFICER'S COLLAR & SLEEVE INSIGNIA —

original 69 members were students of Washington College, Lexington, and the commander was their old Greek teacher.

The recruitment of Negro troops for the Union army was attended by much hesitation and many doubts; it should not be assumed that a desire to free the slaves automatically produced in Northern breasts a feeling of equality. The first units were organised by General David Hunter in the summer and autumn of 1862, from free Negroes and emancipated slaves in the occupied areas of South Carolina and Louisiana. Nomenclature was an embarrassing problem, evaded by the eventual use of the title 'Corps d'Afrique' for the Negro division. Later still the nettle was grasped, and they were designated in the style '4th Regiment, US Colored Troops'. Some 185,000 Negroes are thought to have served in the Union army, of whom some 4,300 became battlefield casualties.

The usual weapon of the infantry of the day was the rifled percussion-lock musket, a muzzle-loading weapon for which pre-measured cartridges wrapped in paper or skin were carried in a large pouch. The copper percussion caps, which were slipped on to a protruding nipple on the outside of the breech, were carried separately. Both rifled and smoothbore weapons were used, and many types of ammunition had to be provided for the variety of makes and calibres. The generic term for bullets, both true balls and conical types, was 'Minie-ball', after the designer of one of the most common systems, the Frenchman Claude Etienne Minié. The most common calibre was .58, that of the Government pattern rifled musket of 1861, but all calibres between .36 and .69 were used. Imported weapons were used by both sides, and in the South rebel arsenals copied the Springfield and Colt designs freely. The Springfield's performance may be taken as typical; it could kill at 1,000 yards, though the chances of hitting anything smaller than a closely-ordered body of men at such ranges were minimal. At 500 or 600 yards it was effective, and at the usual battle ranges of 200 to 300 yards it was deadly. Limb wounds were massive and splintered, usually requiring amputation.

Repeating magazine rifles, breech-loaders firing metallic cartridges, were used in the Civil War in small numbers – some states supplied their Union volunteer units with the Henry rifle, which was devastating against formed troops. Repeating carbines such as the .56 Spencer were more common. A wide variety of cavalry carbines and pistols were used by the mounted troops of both sides, both home-produced and imported British and French weapons. After the Spencer the best carbines were the .56 Sharps and the Burnside.

It should be pointed out, however, that standards of marksmanship among the often sketchily trained soldiers were generally low. It has been calculated that for every man killed or wounded at the First Battle of Bull Run between 8,000 and 10,000 rounds of small arms ammunition were fired. Three aimed shots in one minute was a high rate of fire for a period rifled musket. The socket bayonets universally carried by both sides were, surprisingly, seldom used for their intended purpose. They saw more service as cooking utensils than as weapons.

In the cavalry the sabre was still carried and widely used in action, particularly by Union troops, although by the later stages of the war it was recognised that the ability of cavalry to deploy at speed and then fight dismounted with repeating carbines was at least as important as the traditional sabre charge. In this respect the Union cavalry of 1864-65 was probably the most advanced in the world. One regiment of lancers saw action, the Union's 6th Pennsylvania – 'Rush's Lancers'; the lance was a conspicuous failure and was abandoned in 1863.

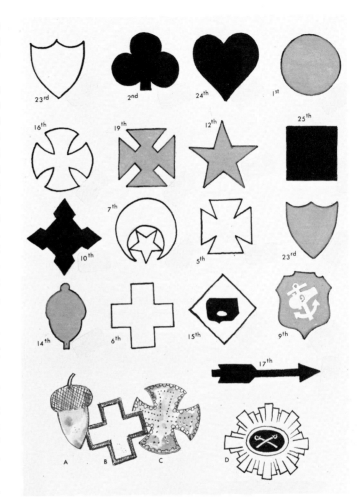

Corps badges of the Union Army, first introduced on an organised basis by General Hooker in 1863. In each Corps the 1st Division patch was red, the 2nd white, the 3rd blue, and the 4th green or orange. 'A' and 'C' are examples of metal Corps badges; 'B' is an officer's badge, edged with gold thread. 'D' is the badge of Sheridan's Cavalry Corps. All badges were generally worn on top of the *kepi* or on the front of the slouch hat. *Artist's Collection*

97

56. Corporal of Union cavalry, 1861

In 1861 the pre-war regular cavalry was reorganised. The old 1st Dragoons became the 1st Cavalry, and the 2nd Dragoons, Mounted Riflemen, and 1st and 2nd Cavalry became the 2nd to 5th Cavalry respectively. At the same time a 6th Cavalry regiment was raised, and the strength of a regiment was increased to six squadrons of two troops of (officially) one hundred men each. Each regiment was commanded by a colonel, with a lieutenant-colonel and three majors, and adjutant, quartermaster and commissary lieutenants on the regimental staff. Each troop was commanded by a captain, with a first and a second lieutenant under him, and sometimes an 'extra' lieutenant as well. Each troop had a first sergeant, five sergeants, and eight corporals; there was one sergeant major per regiment. This structure was followed, loosely, in Confederate regiments as well, but on both sides it varied according to local conditions, and in the southern armies particularly.

This corporal wears the fatigue or forage cap, almost universal field dress in the Union armies, distinguished by a brass badge on the crown comprising crossed sabres beneath the regimental number and above the squadron letter. Photographs show that there were many variations in the cut of this cap, which was originally inspired by the French *casquette d'Afrique* or *képi*. French styles of dress – and facial hair – were extremely fashionable in this period. The short shell jacket trimmed with the yellow lace of the cavalry had been in use, virtually unchanged, since the 1830s; the brass shoulder scales were worn in action early in the war but were generally discarded quite quickly. The sky-blue kersey trousers, reinforced on the inner leg and with a yellow outer stripe, are conventional. There were many types of boot, and many styles of wearing them, from narrow patterns worn under the trousers to thigh-high soft-tops reminiscent of 16th Century cavaliers.

The universal swordbelt specified in the pre-war regulations supports the sabre, which is the long, straight, Prussian style with a brass hilt and a steel scabbard. Later in the war a curved 'Light Cavalry' style was generally adopted. The waistbelt also carries the small pouch for percussion caps, and the 'hog-leg' revolver holster. Several patterns of revolver were used by the Union armies, and in this, as in all other matters of dress and equipment, volunteer regiments tended to present a rather more varied picture than the regulars; but the most common weapons were the Colt's Army .44 and the Remington revolver of the same calibre. The cartridge box for carbine ammunition was worn on the back of the belt. The carbine itself was attached by a ring and snap-hook to the shoulder belt. Among the types issued were the Sharps, Spencer and Burnside; muzzle- and breech-loaders, single-shot and repeating weapons were all used.

57. First Sergeant of Union infantry, 1863

The senior NCO in an infantry company consisting – officially but rarely in fact – of one captain, one first and one second lieutenant, one first sergeant, four sergeants, eight corporals, two musicians, one wagoner, and eighty-two privates. The forage cap is marked with the bugle-horn of the infantry and a company letter, worn on the crown in brass. The field uniform is basically the pre-war fatigue dress with added insignia; a 'sack' coat and sky-blue trousers, with laced shoes. The brass-buttoned coat has the rank chevrons sewn to each sleeve in the branch colour, and the trousers have a dark blue stripe down the outer seam. Rank is also indicated by the red sash and straight, brass-hilted sword worn by all sergeants. The latter is suspended on a single shoulder belt with a circular 'eagle' plate; and sergeants' waistbelts were fitted with a rectangular buckle bearing the national arms, rather than the oval 'US' buckle worn by lower ranks.

The percussion cap pouch for the 1861 Springfield Rifled Musket is worn on the front of the belt to the right of the buckle. Lower ranks carried a large cartridge box behind the right hip, hung on a shoulderbelt over the left shoulder, with the same circular plate as the sergeant illustrated. Sergeants, to avoid having to wear two shoulderbelts, carried the cartridge box on the back of the waistbelt. This NCO has removed his knapsack and blanket, and wears the reduced equipment which he would carry into actual combat. A haversack of proofed material and a cloth-covered tin canteen are slung on shoulder straps to hang on the left hip; the bayonet scabbard hung from the belt in a frog under the haversack. A mug was often slipped on to the canteen stopper chain or the carrying strap.

58. Rifleman, 1st United States ('Berdan's') Sharpshooters, 1863

The 1st and 2nd Sharpshooters, led by General Hiram Berdan, were picked marksmen, largely recruited from the Eastern states. To be considered for this unit the applicant had to place '... at 600 feet distance, ten consecutive shots at an average of five inches from the bull's eye.' The Sharpshooters distinguished themselves in several major engagements, including Gettysburg. They wore one of the more interesting variations on the Union uniform.

The forage cap is of conventional cut, but, like the frock coat and trousers, is of dark green wool. For formal dress a black ostrich plume was added, and a badge consisting of crossed rifles beneath the letters 'US' and over the letters 'SS' has been illustrated. This rifleman wears the red diamond patch of the 1st Division, III Corps on his cap. The coat has a small standing collar and brass buttons at front, cuffs and tail. The trousers are tucked into the socks in the almost universal fashion followed in the field by both sides; some units were issued canvas leggings but they were not widely used. The Sharpshooters were issued with a grey greatcoat trimmed with green. Rank chevrons are reported to have been green on a blue ground.

The knapsack, again, has been discarded, and the soldier carries his necessary effects in his haversack and in the horseshoe-rolled grey issue blanket. The conventional enlisted men's 'US' belt buckle is worn. The rifle he carries is the excellent .52 Sharps single-shot breech-loader, quicker to fire and easier to load in cramped conditions than the .58 Springfield. Initially Berdan's men were issued the .56 Colt's Revolving Rifle, a five-shot weapon with a revolving cylinder like that of the Colt pistol; the greater volume of fire possible with this rifle was largely negated by its unreliability – poorly sealed, it frequently 'cooked off' more than one chamber when fired, with disastrous results to the firer's left hand.

A few picked marksmen in Union formations were issued heavy and meticulously manufactured sniper's rifles, often with telescopic sights. When loaded with scrupulous care and handled by experienced men, these weapons were capable of consistent twelve-inch twenty round groups at ranges of half a mile, and individual results were often far better.

59. Sergeant, 14th New York State Militia, Union army, 1861-64

The French fashion in military styles led to

many colourful uniforms among both Union and Confederate volunteers, more or less closely based on the *zouave* and *chasseur* patterns. In most cases these romantic uniforms – described by eye-witnesses as being of poor workmanship and distinctly tawdry – disappeared relatively early in the war, as state supply arrangements failed to keep up with wear and tear. Some units, however, took great pride in their uniforms and insisted on wearing them right through the war; contemporary accounts speak of the 'red legged *zouaves*' of the 14th Brooklyn at Antietam and Gettysburg.

In fact the 14th wore a *chasseur* uniform – such units as 'Duryea's Zouaves' and the 'Louisiana Tiger Rifles' were distinguished by the unique *zouave* frogging on the short jacket and by fez and turban headgear. The NCO illustrated, the 'Right General Guide' carrying one of the flank marking flags by which men kept their dressing in action, wears a forage cap of conventional cut but with red sides and a red disc on the crown. The short blue jacket has two rows of buttons which are purely decorative – it was sewn to the front of the red vest and could not itself be buttoned. All enlisted ranks wore the detachable red shoulder knots and the broad reversed chevrons in red at the cuffs. Rank chevrons were also in red. A state device is worn on the cap pouch, and the belt buckle is a state issue – 'SNY' for State of New York, sometimes interpreted by rebel wits as standing for 'Snotty Nosed Yank'. Officers are believed to have worn the normal officers' blue frock coat and the regiment's red trousers with a gold outer stripe. The white canvas leggings buttoned down the outside.

60. Sergeant of Heavy Artillery, Corps d'Afrique, Union army, New Orleans, 1863

The Negro division in New Orleans included a regiment of Heavy Artillery who manned some of the massive fixed defences of the Union bastion; this *Corps d'Afrique* sergeant wears the unit's full dress uniform. It was a relatively quiet sector, and ceremonial played a larger part in the duties of the garrison than it did among more exposed troops. (This feature of garrison duty in the great Union centres caused some concern; late in the war General Grant, feeling with some justice that units manning the huge siege pieces in the entrenchments around Washington were making too much of a meal of their soft posting, had them transferred to the front as infantry. The order is reported to have been greeted with glee by other troops.)

The uniform is very similar to that illustrated in **54**, Plate 11. The frock coat is trimmed at collar and cuff in artillery red, and the branch colour is repeated in the trouser stripe, the rank chevrons, and the cords on the Hardee hat. The latter has the usual parade plume, gold eagle pin, and crossed cannons and battery letter. The brass shoulder scales are worn, and an interesting branch variation is provided by the sidearm. This is the Foot Artillery Sword of 1833, copied from a French style which was itself inspired by the old Roman *gladius.*

61. Private of Confederate artillery, 1862

The uniforms of the Southern armies presented a fairly motley appearance from the first days of the war. Although clearly defined uniform regulations were issued in June 1861, practical conditions prevented true uniformity. In all types of unit it was common to see mixtures – dictated by availability or sturdy individual preference – of regulation dress, pre-war state militia uniform, captured Union clothing with new insignia, and frankly home-made garments. Shortages began to bite early on, and the situation degenerated rapidly.

The forage cap was the regulation headgear, with a dark blue band and the sides and crown in the branch colour – red for artillery, pale blue for infantry, yellow for cavalry. The slouch hat was always preferred by the Confederate troops, and the forage cap seems only to have been worn by a minority in practice. Cap insignia were various, and by no means universally worn. This artilleryman wears the regulation forage cap with a small brass crossed cannons badge, copied from a contemporary photograph, but he should not be regarded as typical – *no* Confederate uniform can be regarded as typical. The short grey jacket trimmed in artillery red is also copied from an eyewitness account, but was not regulation issue. (The grey shell jacket, initially worn only by the cavalry, became a popular item of dress in most branches, when obtainable. It was usually worn buttoned at the throat only.) The sky-blue trousers were regulation dress for all branches, and were frequently obtained from captured Union stocks. Footwear was too various to describe.

This soldier carries two items of a field gun crew's equipment; the combined sponge and rammer wielded by the 'Number One', and the gunner's haversack sometimes carried by the 'Number Five'. It has expanding gussets in the sides, and was used to carry cartridges

from the limber to the gun – when it was available, and if there was time to bother with such niceties of safety precautions when under fire.

62. Corporal of Confederate infantry, 1861-62

This NCO wears almost-regulation dress and equipment. General Order No 9 issued by the Adjutant and Inspector-General's Office in Richmond on June 6th, 1861 specified that enlisted men should wear a double-breasted tunic reaching to mid-thigh, 'of gray cloth, known as cadet gray . . . collars and cuffs to be of the colour prescribed for facings for the respective arms of service, and the edges of the tunic to be trimmed throughout with the same colored cloth.' Confederate buttons, of yellow metal, bore the initial letter of the branch – I for infantry, A for artillery, and so forth. The sky blue trousers, made loose 'to spread well over the foot', were worn by regimental officers and all enlisted ranks. Rank chevrons were worn in the branch colour.

The waistbelt is fastened with a rectangular brass buckle with a 'CSA' cypher, and carries the cap pouch, the ammunition box, and the bayonet frog. A linen haversack is slung on the left hip, with a wooden canteen; both metal and wooden styles were used. The Confederacy used a vast number of different types of guns; Government weapons seized from Federal arsenals, copies of Federal weapons made by Southern manufacturers, and imported types. The Government pattern Springfield, in various pirated or captured versions, was the most common, but British Enfields shipped in through the Union blockade were also used in great numbers. The great variety of ammunition sizes and patterns required to feed this diverse collection of firearms put enormous strains on the Confederacy's strictly limited industrial capacity.

63. Lieutenant of Virginia cavalry, Confederate army, 1863

This young Southern cavalier, inspecting his handiwork after target practice with his new Lefaucheaux .41 calibre pin-fire revolver, is representative of the hard-riding regiments which Jeb Stuart led to immortality. The long hair and slouch hat are typical of the period; plumes and feathers were often worn in the hat at the whim of the owner. The short shell jacket in washed-out grey has the regulation yellow collar and cuffs of the Confederate cavalry, and the collar bears the two bars of a first lieutenant (other rank markings are illustrated in the line drawings which accompany this chapter). The elaborate cuff braiding, widely known as 'chicken guts', was authorised for all Confederate officers, on long tunic and shell jacket alike. The shape of the loops was constant for all commissioned ranks; lieutenants, captains, field officers and generals wore one, two, three and four-strand braiding respectively. A popular type of trouser among Southern cavalry officers', was a hard-wearing corduroy, which faded almost to white after frequent washing. A wide variety of high boots were worn, and this style, with a high flap to protect the knee, were popular. The belt is fastened with a circular Virginia state buckle. The Confederate cavalry abandoned sabres earlier than their Yankee counterparts, not least because of the inevitable shortages. Carbines and pistols of every possible type were carried, and in the absence of carbines sawn-off double-barrel muzzle-loading shotguns were found to be most effective in close actions.

The Confederate cavalry regiment was organised along similar lines to the Union formations, though company strength was often nearer fifty than a hundred. Between two and six regiments would be organised into a brigade, and between two and six brigades formed a division. Two or three divisions formed a corps. It was a feature of the Confederate army that while regimental strengths might be comparatively lower, divisional strengths were usually much higher than in the Union forces, through a policy of assigning larger numbers of component units. This was the case in all branches.

64. Private, Woodis Rifles, Virginia militia, Confederate army, 1861
A representative of the fancy militia uniforms which were to be seen in the Confederate lines early in the war. The Woodis Rifles, a militia company raised in 1858 in Norfolk, Virginia, were named after a late mayor of that city. One of five militia companies forming the 3rd Battalion, 54th Regiment of Virginia Militia, the Rifles were called out on April 18th, 1861; when the 6th Virginia Regiment was organised the company was absorbed as C Company. Typically, the company's musicians were remarkably impressive, and they became the regimental band. The Rifles served throughout the Civil War; they fought in the Seven Days Battles around Richmond in the spring of 1862, and were in action from that point until

the surrender at Appomattox. The uniform illustrated probably lasted until it wore out, and it is doubtful if it was replaced.

The uniform of dark hunting green is faced and trimmed with black velvet, with gold spherical buttons and lavish gold cord decoration. The trousers have a black velvet welt edged with gold cord. The black felt Hardee hat is turned up on the left, and is decorated with a gold cord, a red hackle, and a gold-on-black bugle-horn badge beneath 'WR'; these initials are repeated on the belt buckle.

65. Confederate infantryman, 1864
An eloquent testimony to the plight of the Southern armies in the last two years of the war is the fact that the great battle of Gettysburg began as a shoe-hunting expedition – after the initial clashes at a low level both sides reinforced the troops on the scene until mutual escalation led to one of the bloodiest battles of the war. This 'Johnny Reb' is anxiously examining the split wooden sole of his 'utility' shoe; nailed leather and wood brogans were common Confederate wear in the absence of sufficient shoe leather.

His jacket and trousers are home-dyed 'butternut'; every conceivable cut, and every shade of grey and brown from off-white to dark chestnut were to be seen in the Southern ranks in the late stages of the war. His equipment has been reduced to a simple belt with cap-pouch and cartridge box, and a horseshoe roll wrapped in a captured Yankee 'gum blanket' – a rubber-muslin compound with a slit in the middle which was used as a rainproof poncho. Slouch hats of many patterns and colours were worn. The absence of proper field equipment was often due to personal choice as much as to shortages. The Confederate often deliberately discarded all but the bare minimum, preferring to risk missing dumped kit rather than carry articles he might never use. This habit sometimes reached extremes, with canteens and even cartridge boxes being thrown away; it was held that a good tin mug was more useful than a canteen, as it could be used for both drinking and cooking, and that ammunition was handier if kept loose in the pockets. Greatcoats, if they were ever issued, were often thrown away in summer, in the confident belief that some sort of replacement could be found when the weather turned. Magnificent in battle, the Southern soldier was often an improvident campaigner.

PLATE 12

56

58

57

59

60

PLATE 13

61

63

64

62

65

6 The Years of Confidence

The meeting of Lee and Grant at Appomattox on April 9th, 1865 left the United States with a magnificent army, probably second to none in the world. The rapid demobilisation of 'duration only' troops cut the strength of the Army of the Republic to 57,000 in little more than a year, but it was still a formidable force which could look forward to the possibility of operations against a first class European power with confidence. But Sheridan's sabre-rattling in Texas served its purpose, and France, embroiled in a political adventure in Mexico, chose to back down when a face-saving opportunity presented itself. The US Army now faced only two enemies, but both of them were deadly – the Indian, and the Washington establishment.

The latter of these two foes proved the deadliest. The war was won, the nation was exhausted and desperate to turn to the work of reconstruction, and armies were expensive. In 1869 the standing army was cut to 39,000 men; in 1873, with four years more occupation duty in the South to carry out and the frontier seething, it was further reduced to 25,000. This force was expected to enforce the edicts of Washington, to police vast areas where civilian law and order hardly existed even in name, to repair by crude surgery the hideous damage done by the venal and inadequate Bureau of Indian Affairs, and to guard the Republic's frontiers from the Canadian border to the Rio Grande, from the banks of the Missouri to the beaches of the Pacific – this, in a period when the great Westward surge of the Eastern and immigrant pioneers reached its fullest flood.

The final confrontation of red man and white was coming, and when the immovable object stood in the way of the irresistible force it was the tiny frontier army which had to find a solution. The shame of America's war of

By the early years of the 20th Century the khaki tropical service uniform prescribed in 1898 was at last reaching the troops. It is seen here worn by a US Marine stationed in China in the aftermath of the Boxer Rising. This photograph captures well the neat, essentially modern appearance of the uniform. Note the Krag rifle, the 1902 webbing cartridge pouches and belt, and the USMC badge pinned to the campaign hat.

A trooper of the US 1st Cavalry in field dress, photographed in the 1890s. In some ways his appearance has changed remarkably little from that of his predecessors of Custer's day; the slouch hat, 'sack' coat, kersey trousers, high-fronted boots and bandana all recall the Indian Wars. The leather sabre-belt with its cap-and-ball revolver in a 'hog-leg' holster have given place to a fabric cartridge belt and a Colt Peacemaker, however. *US Signal Corps.*

extinction on the Indians has been well documented; less well appreciated is the fact that the army itself had less to be ashamed about than its political masters. That there were occasional shameful episodes, such as the Sand Creek Massacre, is a matter of record. It could be argued, however, that these were balanced by the barbarism of the tribes towards white men, women and (on occasion) children in numerous terrible incidents. The real shame of America in this period must be borne by the Bureau of Indian Affairs, by uncaring and cynical politicians, and by ruthless commercial interests.

The army which, as the only force on the spot, had to bear the burden of these thankless campaigns bore very little resemblance to the image since created by the fantasists of Hollywood. There were never more than 15,000 men available on the frontier, to control an area of a million square miles – one man to every fifty square miles. The extraordinary thing is that, given the magnitude and ugliness of their task, their sense of neglect and abandonment, and their miserable conditions, this tiny force managed to maintain a remarkably high morale and level of professional skill. They were cynical, embittered, and frustrated – and out of their very sense of frustration they forged a defiant spirit. They ceased to expect understanding or support from Washington, and prided themselves in their self-sufficiency.

The end of the Civil War found the army with just six cavalry regiments. Since even Washington was able to appreciate that the vast distances of the South-West demanded the mobility of mounted troops, this figure was increased to ten in late 1866. The 9th and 10th Cavalry were composed of Negro soldiers with white officers – the famous 'Buffalo Soldiers' – so nicknamed by the Indians because their kinky hair resembled the curly skull of the

106

bison. By 1870 the general 'spheres of influence' of the regiments had settled down, with the 1st, 3rd and 8th Cavalry in Nevada, Arizona and New Mexico, the 2nd and 5th in Nebraska, Wyoming and Montana, the 7th in Kansas, and the 4th, 6th, 9th and 10th in Texas.

The calibre of the officers varied sharply from unit to unit throughout the army. There were dedicated and skilful officers who carried out their thankless task with as much imagination and humanity as the conditions allowed; there were also self-important martinets and glory-hunters whose personal ambitions outweighed a proper care of their men. Both types found plenty of scope for their talents in the isolated posts scattered throughout the wilderness. The possibilities for promotion and advancement for an officer in a frontier regiment were extremely limited – the army was too small and competition was too great. This was an undesirable situation much aggravated by the number of officers who, after rising to high command at very young ages during the Civil War, found themselves relegated to junior substantive ranks. It is hard to adjust oneself to the change from a Brigadier-General's command in major battles, to a Captaincy in a one-company mud-brick post thousands of miles from civilisation, defending an arid wilderness against a few hundred elusive tribesmen. Many failed to make the adjustment. Some, hungry to make a name for themselves which would return them to what they regarded as their proper level of responsibility, were guilty of disastrous errors of judgement – witness one George Armstrong Custer.

The neglect from which these dedicated, often grey-haired lieutenants and captains suffered may be judged by the fact that in 1876, the year of the Battle of Little Big Horn, the fifty-fourth Congress of the United States

Infantry officer's shako, of the type worn between 1872 and 1881. The branch insignia changed from the bugle-horn to the crossed rifles (woven here in gold wire, below the regimental number) in 1875. *From the collection of Gerald H. Miller*

Model 1881 helmet for officers of US Infantry. *From the collection of Gerald H. Miller*

of America adjourned without bothering to pass the Appropriations Act for the coming year. Consequently, the United States Army was not payed until November 1877. The men at least had their free issue rations; the officers, expected to pay for their food, had to exist as best they could! The standard of skill, application, and serious work towards national policy objectives displayed by the various staff bureaux in the War Department has been described as too appalling for a sane officer to grasp.

The army which suffered the direction of these 'staff officers' was tough, spare, and capable. The troopers were a mixture of pre-war regulars (by now the survivors would have risen to NCO rank in almost all cases, explaining the taut discipline and high professional standards of most units), recent immigrants who could hardly speak the language, ruined ex-Confederates, drifters, drunks and assorted hard cases. They enlisted for five years at a time, for a wage of $16:00 per month – *reduced* to $13:00 in 1872! A company officer, perhaps a decorated veteran of the Civil War who had once had 3,000 sabres under his command, now served out his time in the wilderness on $125:00 per month, from which he had to feed, clothe and raise his family and buy his own uniforms, weapons, horses and saddlery.

The men got little training, being expected to learn the necessary skills of horsemanship and musketry during their first few months of service on an operational post. Ammunition was often so restricted that a man might be allocated one dozen rounds per year for target practice. The diet was drab in the extreme – salt beef or pork, dried fish, beans, rice, hardtack, and the terrifying army coffee reputed to be capable of 'growing whiskers on a cannon ball.' This might be supplemented by

Ogden print of officers and an enlisted man in the 'winter field dress' of the 1880s. The officers' greatcoats, one with a cape buttoned to it, are richly frogged and knotted with black silk, in a manner reminiscent of Confederate officers' 'chicken-guts'. The *kepi* badges reflect both unit and branch; the officer on the left wears the staff badge, a wreathed US cypher. The cavalryman wears the grey-blue caped overcoat, with the cape extending to the wrists, which had been in use since the Civil War by mounted troops. *US National Archives*

Group of Negro soldiers of the 25th Infantry—'Carpenter's Brunettes'—photographed in the dress uniform of the 1880s. Note the white collars, shoulder straps, piping, and NCO's chevrons and trouser stripes; and the spiked Model 1881 helmet. The two soldiers on the left in frogged coats are musicians. *US Signal Corps*

Enlisted men's shako and *kepi* insignia, 1872-1890s. In the centre are the Infantry shako eagle and bugle-horn worn from 1872 to 1875, in which year the horn was replaced by the crossed rifles (bottom left). The bugle-horn (bottom right) was retained for musicians, however. (Top left) and (top right) are the *kepi* insignia of the Cavalry and Artillery. *David Scheinmann*

Fascinating print which captures a meeting between General George Crook (second from right) and Geronimo, leader of the renegade Chiricahua Apaches (left hand man in squatting group in middleground). The photograph was taken by an enterprising cameraman named C. S. Fly, of Tombstone, Arizona. The council took place on March 25th, 1886, in the Canon de los Embudos, Sonora. Note the great variety of dress worn by the white men, including Crook's strange and unbecoming sun helmet. In the centre of the sitting figures can be seen an Indian scout wearing an Army coat with sergeant major's chevrons. Apache warriors, in their traditional kilts and breech-clouts, may be seen in the background. *Radio Times Hulton Picture Library*

vegetables grown on the post, but in many cases the soil and climate were too arid to raise anything nutritious. Apart from officers' wives and a handful of washerwomen, a soldier might not see a woman for years at a time. Discipline was extremely harsh, facilities for any recreation except hard drinking virtually non-existent, and disease rampant despite the best efforts to maintain standards of hygiene. The service demanded that men spend long days in the saddle under a blazing sun, jogging endlessly through harsh terrain on month-long patrols or escort details, with the constant possibility of attack by a wily, courageous and hideously cruel enemy. The Indian brave is generally conceded to have been the finest light cavalryman the world has produced; hardened from birth by his harsh environment, a master of concealment and ambush, able to cover incredible distances on foot or pony, able to keep himself and his mount alive and in fighting trim in a land which to a white man seemed to offer not the slightest sustenance. Desertions were a constant drain on manpower; one US Government source stated that of the men recruited between 1867 and 1891 one-third deserted.

This was the army which fought more than 900 separate engagements between 1865 and the final, depressing encounter at Wounded Knee, South Dakota, as 1890 drew to a close. Seen in context, its shortcomings are hardly surprising, its moments of glory doubly impressive.

While the frontier army shouldered the white man's burden, the country which pre-

ferred not to think about them was moving inexorably towards the status of a world power. The enormous influx of immigrants, the industrial advances and commercial exploitation of a vast sub-continent, the huge fortunes which were made and lost and made again tenfold – all the symptoms of a vigorous, lusty, growing society were to be observed. Despite the self-conscious determination to remain aloof from the Old World which was still widely preached – and which would continue to command enormous political support until 1942 – it was inevitable that this thrusting young power should eventually face, and as inevitably overwhelm, the last vestiges of old-style imperialism in the New World. The clash, when it finally came, would free the enlisted soldier from the cynical neglect of incompetents and the

swindling of profiteers in a surprisingly short time; such are the marvels of a hard-nosed Press and a well-informed public. Many a leathery veteran of the Indian Wars must have smiled bitterly.

The short Spanish-American War was one of those conflicts for which the ostensible reason seems unconvincing; quite simply, it occurred because it was time for it to occur. Newly conscious of their strength and national identity, inspired by a jingoist spirit and frankly aching to try out their new muscle, the population inundated the reception centres when the call went out for volunteers to supplement the 30,000 regulars in service in 1898. Within a few months 200,000 men had answered the call. The sizes of companies were increased, a third battalion was added to each regiment,

and still they came; the system was hopelessly inadequate to cope with them, of course, and the supply, transport and general administration services broke down before the war had properly begun.

The United States armed forces are today a byword for lavish and carefully designed equipment, swarming service and support units, swift transportation, and the high level of personal comfort accorded to the combat soldier whenever humanly possible; indeed, this emphasis on the soldier's comfort has been criticized on several occasions as encouraging 'softness'. In this context it is strange to reflect that it was in all these areas of military life that America was most deficient at the turn of the century. Compared to the British 'Tommy' serving the Widow of Windsor on

Anson Mills cartridge belt plate of the US 7th Cavalry, 1881. *Hinton/Robson*

Indian Scout's helmet, 1890. The Cavalry eagle plate has crossed arrows superimposed on the central shield; the cords and cap lines are red and white, and there are four red strands in the white plume. *From the collection of Gerald H. Miller*

Full dress uniforms displayed by a group of US Army generals and staff officers at the time of the Spanish American War.

A US infantry squad in field dress, 1898. Note the white chevrons and trouser-stripes. The two officers wear the 1895 dark blue undress tunic trimmed with black mohair braiding, with swords slung from an interior belt. The soldiers wear blue 'sack' coats, and full field equipment including khaki canvas leggings. All ranks wear khaki campaign hats and sky-blue trousers. The rifles are the new .30 calibre Krag-Jorgensen magazine rifles.

the Indian North-West Frontier, the American soldier in Cuba was shamefully treated. The transport from Tampa, Florida, to Cuba was organised through civilian contractors; the rapacity of these patriots was only equalled by the squalor and inefficiency of their vessels. The rapidly-assembled army found itself blundering through the jungle at the mercy of hopeless staff preparation. Standards of sanitation were not high among the Volunteers, and in the unhealthy climate disease soon ran through the army like a brush-fire. The water was often putrid, but the men had not been educated on the dangers and no proper provision had been made to supply them with safe water; dysentery, cholera and typhoid joined malaria and yellow fever in the Spanish armoury.

The food deemed proper for the support of this brave, keen, gay young citizen-army in a tropical jungle campaign consisted of sow-belly (which was exactly what it sounds like), hard-tack and canned 'beef'. This latter was offal,

pure and simple; the present writer has decided, on humanitarian grounds, to spare the reader a detailed description, which has been published elsewhere, from a soldier's letter home.

The standard of generalship was hardly higher than the standard of supply and rationing; nevertheless, the troops aquitted themselves very creditably. The famous charge at San Juan Hill, the strongly fortified position defending the landward side of the Spanish-occupied port of Santiago, has passed into folklore. The units involved were the 'Rough Riders' of Teddy Roosevelt's 1st US Volunteer Cavalry, the 6th and 16th Infantry, and the 1st and 10th regular Cavalry (the latter still composed of 'Buffalo Soldiers'). On July 17th, only three months after war was declared, Santiago was surrendered to the obese General Shafter – who had been forced to move about his command by buckboard rather than on horseback, in view of his build. After the cheering, the ecstatic editorials, the ceremonial

welcome for the returning heroes, came the post-mortem; 385 soldiers had been killed in action and more than 5,000 had died of wounds and disease. A Congressional Committee got to work. The Secretary of War was forced to resign, a War College was founded, and, in due course, a long-overdue General Staff. The supply and medical services were completely rebuilt by dedicated officers, and the sharp lessons of Cuba were taken to heart throughout the armed forces. It was not lost on investigators that the US Marines, who operated at Guantanamo during the campaign, had an incomparably better record of health and supply than the army; most of their officers were experienced in tropical campaigning, and took a serious professional pride in caring for

their men. Indifference at a high level, and simple ignorance at a low level, would no longer be tolerated.

Between 1899 and 1901 a brutal, wearying and obscure campaign was fought in the Philippines. Natives who had taken advantage of the landing of American troops to rise against their Spanish masters now turned on the new-comers, when it became clear that they had merely exchanged one master for another. It was a campaign of exhausting jungle patrols, swift ambushes and as swift retreats, and bloody night raids. Among the officers who distinguished themselves was a Captain John J. Pershing.

By the time this officer's name came to the notice of the public at large once more, the US

'The Forgotten Fifteenth"—the US 15th Infantry—remained at Tiensin in China for many years, long after the international situation suggested any overt reason for their presence. These soldiers of the regiment, photographed in about 1910, wear the 1902 olive drab service uniform.

Army had changed radically. The reforms which followed the Cuban scandal had taken effect.

In 1910 the Mexican President Diaz abdicated, and that unhappy country was once more torn by revolution and factional warfare. Pancho Villa, vigorously anti-American, led one such powerful faction, and anxiety for the safety of American lives and property increased. Matters came to a head in 1916 when Villa crossed the border and raided the town of Columbus, New Mexico; a brisk battle took place in the main street of the town between the Mexican raiders and men of the 13th US Cavalry. A powerful punitive expedition was at once organised under the command of Brigadier-General John J. Per-

shing. With the grudging acquiescence – but without the co-operation – of the Mexican Government, Pershing set up headquarters in the state of Chihuahua and sent out several cavalry columns in an attempt to capture Villa dead or alive. This he failed to do, but in the course of several successful engagements with the guerillas he clearly demonstrated American superiority, inflicting quite large losses including one of Villa's most important lieutenants. One skirmish began and finished in a matter of seconds, with a junior officer of the 8th Cavalry dropping three ambushing *Villistas* from their saddles with three shots from his pistol. Lieutenant George S. Patton was never to lose his fondness for pistols.

PLATE 14

66

68

69

67

70

PLATE 15

71

72

73

74

75

PLATE 16

76

77

78

79

80

66. Sergeant-Major, 9th United States Cavalry, full dress, 1875

In the latter half of the 19th Century armies the world over still reflected in their dress the extravagance of the Napoleonic Wars, complicated by various native conventions copied during the great colonial expansions of the period. It is hardly surprising, therefore, that the United States Army should have adopted a full dress uniform more elaborate than any it had worn before. This new rig appeared in 1872, displaying several features plainly inspired by current European styles.

This NCO, the senior enlisted man in his regiment, wears the uniform as it would have appeared around 1875; life in the Indian-fighting cavalry was as remarkable for the amount of 'spit and polish' demanded when on post as for the latitude allowed to all ranks when on column. The yellow plume and cords on the black felt helmet indicate the branch; the other mounted branches wore the same helmet with their own branch colour distinctions. The gilt national helmet plate was common to all mounted branches. Officers wore gilt cords, with branch colour plumes. The chinstrap was black leather for all ranks. (Note that the helmet cords extend down to the chest.)

The short-skirted tailored tunic of dark blue has plain shoulder straps, and collar tabs bearing the regimental number in brass, of cavalry yellow cloth. Rank and re-enlistment chevrons, cuff patches and piping are all in the branch colour. This style was common to all enlisted personnel, and the rank chevrons are the only insignia illustrated here which could not equally have been worn by a trooper. The re-enlistment chevrons here indicate one Civil War enlistment and one peacetime re-enlistment.

The pale blue kersey cavalry trousers have a yellow stripe down the out-seam for NCOs; they are worn over black spurred boots. The white 'Berlin' gloves were replaced by gauntlets from about 1885 onwards. The brass-hilted sabre in its white metal scabbard has black leather suspenders and wrist-strap, and a black leather belt is worn with the old Civil War eagle buckle. Officially replaced by a rectangular plate bearing the 'US' cypher in an oval, by an order dated 1872, this older buckle was still to be seen a number of years afterwards. Officers' belts and sabre furniture were of black leather

strapping with gilt thread decoration in lengthways stripes.

Officers wore a simpler tunic, double-breasted with two rows of buttons. There was no yellow piping, the collar was plain and bore no insignia, and the cuff patches were replaced by loops of gilt thread braiding – two loops up to and including captain's rank, three loops for higher ranks. The rear skirt decoration, of quite elaborate pattern and in the branch colour for enlisted men, was also much more restrained on the officer's tunic. Heavy woven gilt shoulder knots were worn, however, bearing markings of rank and the regimental number.

67. Trooper, 7th US Cavalry, campaign dress, 1875

Contemporary material shows that Hollywood's version of the cavalry trooper on campaign is quite erroneous. Surviving photographs and items of dress leave one with the impression that a frontier cavalry troop must have presented a motley appearance indeed. Both officers and men were allowed great latitude in the field, and apparently took full advantage of it.

This trooper of Custer's 7th is remarkably restrained and smart by the standards of the day. Civilian-bought shirts, hats, scarves and weaponry were very widely observed; this soldier has limited his private wardrobe to a bandana. These were almost invariably private purchases, and of every possible colour. The shapeless hat, its black felt weathered to a neutral dark grey, is the ludicrous campaign hat of 1872 issue. It had no resistance to sun or rain, and was provided with hooks and eyes round the brim so that this could be fastened up in the manner of a bicorn cocked hat – otherwise a rain shower sent it sinking dismally round the wearer's head like a soggy hood. Photographs of officers of the 7th in the Dakotas reveal that methods of wearing the hat varied from man to man, and any group bears a distinct resemblance to the cast of a pirate operetta! All ranks tended to wear privately purchased slouch hats, straw hats or forage caps in preference to this unfortunate design.

The tunic is the five-button 'sack' coat issued in 1874; examples with yellow piping round the collar and cuffs were also issued, but disappeared during the 1880s. The shirt, when government issue was worn at all, was a grey pullover type; blue shirts were also issued in smaller numbers. NCOs had the usual yellow stripe down the seam of the sky-blue kersey trousers, which were reinforced with

canvas in the crutch. The heavy, wide-topped spurred boots are typical of the period.

On his waistbelt, still fastened by the old pattern buckle, the trooper carries the holster for his Colt .44 cap-and-ball revolver and the small pouch for its ammunition and primers. On the back of the belt he wears a large leather pouch, perhaps one of those originally designed for percussion ammunition but now altered to take the metal cartridges of his .50 calibre single-shot Springfield carbine. This is normally carried snapped to the hook on his shoulder sling. Privately purchased or made cartridge belts, with loops for carbine ammunition, were often worn. The sabre was usually left with the supply wagons when out on column or patrol.

68. Captain of US Cavalry, campaign dress, 1870s

This officer has abandoned his campaign hat in disgust, and wears his standard pattern forage cap, the front decorated with embroidered sabres and a regimental number. The officers' gold chinstrap did not appear until the 1880s.

His shirt is of the style much favoured by officers of the period – privately purchased and to private specification. It has a plastron front, with fancy yellow piping of a vaguely military appearance around the collar and chest. It is worn with a black cravat. The coat is the standard issue officer's undress 'sack', the sleeves, chest and collar decorated with black silk braiding. The style of braiding was the same for all commissioned ranks. The rank boxes on the shoulders comprise rectangles of cavalry yellow within heavy gold braid borders, with the two bars of captain's rank attached at each end.

The trousers, with officers' style one-and-a-half-inch yellow stripes, are worn tucked into a pair of privately purchased boots. A 'butcher-knife' was commonly carried, often in a sheath decorated with fancy Indian bead or quill work, or with brass tacks.

69. Apache Scout, 1880s

Indian scouts had been used by white soldiers since the earliest period of European settlement in America, but it was not until 1866 that Congress officially sanctioned the practice. During the most savage campaigns of the Indian Wars there were many Indians who served alongside the US Cavalry; it should be remembered that generally speaking these campaigns were not seen by the individual Indian as a racial war between red and white, but as a tribal clash. So long as their tribe was not directly involved in the issue they felt free to join either side, and when they fought with the white man they brought to his armoury their own unflinching courage, savage determination, and enormous skill in fieldcraft.

Generally these scouts were hired on a local basis, and the issue of uniform was a matter for the local commander. Often none was issued, and the scouts wore their traditional dress, or, more often, a combination of native and cast-off European dress. In other cases the full cavalry campaign uniform was issued, but efforts to persuade the scouts to wear the uniform in the regulation manner were totally unavailing. Surviving descriptions of troops of scouts suggest that no two men appeared alike. Many wore odd items of the uniform, modified to suit their own ideas of comfort – usually by cutting the seat out of the breeches. The combination illustrated here may be taken as typical.

The headband is worn in the usual Apache manner, but many scouts added a slouch hat, often with the brass sabres of the cavalry. Over an old civilian shirt is worn a 'sack' tunic – in this case, the nine-button type made from old Civil War frock coats; the uniform garments issued for scouts were often of outdated pattern. As leader of a group of scouts attached to some cavalry troop or company this Apache has been given a corporal's chevrons to mark his status; this sign of authority would appeal to his pride, but he holds his position of leadership by the harsh old criteria of personal strength and cunning rather than by the invested authority of the white soldier. Like many of the scouts he has discarded army trousers – if he ever received them – in favour of the traditional native dress of cloth kilt, breechclout, and buckskin leggings. Moccasins were invariably worn in preference to the white man's boots. He carries an old .50 calibre Springfield carbine, which he has decorated with brass tacks; cartridges are carried in looped waist and cross-belts, and the inevitable knife is thrust in some convenient position.

In 1890, after the fury of the Indian Wars was spent, the scouts were regularised by a general order. The new United States Scouts, enlisting for six months at a time, were issued regular campaign and dress uniforms – the latter, ironically enough, being the most colourful of all the army's dress orders. It was very

similar to that worn by the cavalry (see **66**) but yellow was replaced as the branch colour by mixed white and red. The scout of the 1890s, striding the parade ground of Fort Sill in his tall helmet plumed with white and red horsehair, his blue tunic with its red-piped white collar, shoulder straps and cuff patches, his red-and-white striped blue kersey breeches and his gleaming accoutrements, could hardly be in greater contrast to the scout illustrated here. The new campaign uniform included a long dun-coloured overcoat with a pointed hood for winter and night guard dress; and the crossed sabres were replaced by crossed arrows in white metal with the letters 'USS'.

70. Corporal of US Infantry, 1880
The year 1872 saw the beginning of a period of great experimentation and no little confusion in uniform regulations throughout the US Army.

The infantry received a new dress uniform at the same time as the cavalry (see **66**) and other branches. It consisted of the stiff shako illustrated here, a tunic basically similar to the type worn by the cavalry NCO described above but with rather longer skirts, and sky-blue trousers. The infantry branch colour of light blue appeared in the form of piping around the shako, and the cuff and collar tabs, shoulder straps, tail decoration and piping of the tunic. It was repeated in the rank chevrons. The NCO's trouser stripe was dark blue, since the correct shade would have been almost invisible. The shakos of enlisted men had a white tuft, and those of officers a small plume of white cock feathers. The infantry branch badge was changed from a bugle horn to crossed rifles in 1875. Officers wore a double-breasted coat of longer cut but basically the same design as mounted officers, with the same rank distinctions. The normal undress wear was the familiar *chasseur*-style cap – rather lower in the crown than the Civil War *kepi* – and the rather loose dark blue blouse; several different types were observed, including the style with collar and cuffs piped in the branch colour described above, and a very full cut style falling in vertical pleats.

In 1881 the shako was replaced by a black felt helmet of similar but not identical design to that worn by the cavalry and other mounted troops since 1872. The helmet plate now reflected the branch, and the new style helmet replaced the earlier model in mounted units. In the infantry and other foot branches the enlisted

men wore a helmet with a spiked top; initially officers wore plumes and tassels, but from 1884 all ranks wore the spike. In the same year the branch colour of the infantry changed to white; rank chevrons remained in the relevant facing colour, with black stitching, except on the men's greatcoats. Infantry NCOs wore dark blue chevrons on the greatcoat. 1884 also saw the introduction of a cork pith helmet as summer headgear for the whole army; for the previous five years the troops had been authorised to wear straw hats and white duck trousers in extreme climates. Throughout the last quarter of the century, there was an increased use of slouch hats as campaigning wear by all branches.

71. Major of US Artillery, 1895
This officer wears the dark blue uniform with black mohair braiding decoration introduced in 1895, for 'undress' wear. It was worn in the field, although the blue pillbox cap was frequently replaced by a slouch campaign hat.

The cap bears the national coat of arms, and has a gilt chinstrap and buttons. The collar of the tunic bears the gilt cypher 'US' followed by the branch of service badge, in this case the crossed cannon barrels of the artillery. In the upper bight of the cannon appears the battery letter 'F' and in the lower bight the regimental number. The gold oakleaf of Major's rank appears on the shoulder straps. The black braiding on the tunic follows the edge of the cut-out on the left hip which accommodates the hilt of the sword, when worn; this officer simply has the leather suspender for attachment to the scabbard hanging loose from the interior belt.

72. Private of US Infantry, 1898
The outbreak of the Spanish-American War caught the US Army in a state of transition, and the appearance of the troops reflected this. A khaki field service uniform, to be worn with a khaki campaign hat and canvas gaiters, was authorised in 1898 to replace the dark blue tunic, dark blue shirt and light blue trousers currently in use. The men of the Expeditionary Force, regulars and militiamen alike, displayed every possible combination of the two uniforms. The campaign hat and gaiters seem to have been universal issue, but in the absence of khaki tunics most men wore their dark blue flannel shirts in the field – sometimes with the sleeves cut short – and blue and khaki trousers were worn indiscriminately, simply according to availability. Many officers had received their

khaki uniforms, however. Cork pith helmets were quite widely worn by officers, both white and pale khaki drab versions being observed.

This regular infantryman wears the campaign hat creased into the style he prefers – no two men looked alike in this respect. The brass badge comprises crossed rifles with the regimental number above and the company letter below. His dark blue flannel shirt is worn open for coolness in the swamp country through which he is struggling. His blue kersey trousers are tucked into canvas gaiters. His personal kit has been reduced to a canteen, a haversack, a bayonet, the fabric Mills cartridge belt double-banked to hold ammunition for his .30 calibre 1892 Krag-Jorgensen magazine rifle (with extra ammunition carried in socks tied round his neck!), and his blanket and shelter half in a horseshoe roll containing small personal kit.

The haversack is stencilled with the crossed rifles, regimental number and company letter, over the national cypher. The horseshoe roll was universally preferred as field equipment to the fussy and over-complicated back pack of the period. The Merriam pack was apparently one of those items known to every soldier – it was ingenious and carefully designed, but far too complex to be of practical value to a front-line soldier in rough country.

The Krag rifle was in short supply during the war, and generally only regulars were equipped with them. The single-shot .45-70 Springfield was carried by the bulk of the militia regiments, with a single-bank cartridge belt for the larger rounds. Late in the war, in the Philippine theatre, 25 Krags were issued per company to all troops with the older rifles, for use by selected marksmen.

73. Trooper, 1st US Volunteer Cavalry, 1898
The single unit most frequently associated with the Spanish-American War in the public mind is the 1st United States Volunteer Cavalry Regiment – Teddy Roosevelt's 'Rough Riders'. As so frequently occurs, this pride of place is ill-founded in fact. The 1st Volunteer Cavalry were an enthusiastic, hardy outfit who benefited enormously from the patronage of the then Assistant Secretary of the Navy, the colourful and publicity-conscious Theodore Roosevelt. He ensured that his 'Terrors' got the equipment and weapons they needed, and his breezy enthusiasm for the coming fight kept the regiment in the public eye. As Lieutenant-Colonel of the 1st Volunteer Cavalry (he wisely

refused the command in favour of an experienced veteran of the Indian Wars) Roosevelt earned enormous popularity and electoral advantage, and the regiment immortality, in the famous charge up Kettle Hill at San Juan. In Cuba, it should be pointed out, the cavalry fought dismounted.

The 'Rough Riders' were recruited by the Federal Government as distinct from a State administration, in response to a provision in the Congressional bill of 1898 which mobilised volunteers to augment the regular army. This clause called for 3,000 enlistees to be supplied by the Federal Government.

This illustration shows a trooper as he might have appeared at San Antonio during the weeks of training and 'working up' which preceded the regiment's embarkation at Tampa, Florida. The trooper is one of the Western cowboys who made up a high proportion of the regiment's strength – a fact suggested by his preference for 'rolling his own' from the traditional sack of Bull Durham tobacco! As stated above, the new khaki tropical uniform was in short and uncertain supply, and even the wire-pulling of the enthusiastic second in command could not shake enough free from the Federal warehouses to equip his regiment properly. The bulk of the troopers therefore improvised by wearing the light brown canvas or coarse linen stable dress of the cavalry, normally worn as fatigues. This rather ungainly and shapeless jacket and trousers made a reasonable hot-weather combat uniform. Another combination widely seen was the blue flannel uniform shirt worn with the brown trousers. This cowboy wears the stable fatigues over his familiar 'Long Johns'. His campaign hat is worn entirely according to individual taste. He uses the brass cap badge to pin up the front of the brim; these badges were by no means universally worn, and those who had them pinned them to the front or side of the crown or brim indiscriminately. The badge consists of crossed sabres with '1' above and 'USV' below.

The ubiquitous khaki canvas gaiters are worn over regulation boots. The double-row Mills cartridge belt is worn, and as this would not easily accommodate such items as knives, revolver holsters, and so forth, a privately purchased leather belt is worn under it. An army holster accommodates the .30 calibre 1884 Colt six shot revolver. One of Roosevelt's most useful bits of lobbying concerned his regiment's arms. He succeeded in acquiring for them the new magazine carbine – a .30 calibre

Krag-Jorgensen – of the regular cavalry, and this single fact probably accounted for a good measure of their success in action.

74. Corporal, Cuban Volunteer Battalion, 1898
The unrest in Cuba during the last quarter of the 19th Century was one of the elements which persuaded America to go to war. The constant native uprisings became too much for the small regular garrison to cope with; it consisted mainly of the 44th Antillas Infantry Regiment and the 17th Cuba and 18th Habana Rifle Battalions, stiffened by drafts of reinforcements from Spain. To increase the available forces the local government raised large numbers of volunteer battalions from among the local male population, and this branch eventually numbered some 80,000. Its strength was the reason for America's mobilisation of militia regiments in the late 1890s, as it outnumbered the entire US Army establishment of the day by nearly three to one. Trained and armed like the regular forces, these battalions comprised infantry, cavalry, artillery and engineer units, each with a peacetime establishment of about 400 men and a war establishment of 1,000.

The soldier illustrated wears campaign dress, and is rather smarter and more completely equipped than the bulk of these volunteers usually were; Spain provided arms and ammunition, but clothing had to be privately purchased. Payment was inclined to be irregular, and increasingly took the form of a sort of official 'IOU' rather than hard cash.

The straw hat has a black patent leather band and the red-yellow-red cockade of Spain. The blouse and trousers are of washable cotton material in a sort of 'pillow ticking' pattern, known as rayadillo. For garrison and parade dress these were smartened up by the addition of coloured collars and cuffs, trouser stripes, and rank markings. We have chosen to show the rank insignia of a corporal on campaign clothing, but all insignia was usually omitted in the field. The coloured distinctions on the more formal uniform indicated branch – green for infantry, red for all other branches. Rank insignia for all branches comprised three gold or silver stripes for sergeants, three red stripes for corporals, and one red stripe above the elbow for senior privates. Officers were distinguished by complex arrangements of stars and lace stripes on the cuffs, and wore metal gorgets with formal dress.

A variety of leather pouches and harness were

issued, in either black or brown. A grey blanket was usually worn in a horseshoe roll, and a white linen haversack was often issued. The trousers were sometimes gathered into short leather anklets. The rifle is the standard Spanish Army issue of the day, a version of the single-shot 1870 .50 calibre Remington breechloader, widely exported and manufactured under licence abroad. In conclusion it should be mentioned that this dress was also typical of Spanish forces in Puerto Rico and the Philippines.

75. Captain of US Infantry, tropical service dress, 1903
The neat and (by contemporary standards) practical tropical service uniform was in full use by the early years of the 20th Century; this officer is illustrated as he would have appeared on garrison and police duties in the occupied Philippines.

The campaign hat was now universal wear, with cords indicating branch and grade. All officers wore gold cords during this period; the national coat of arms in bronze finish metal was also worn by all officers, on the stand-up collar. The national cypher would replace this once again in a few years time – see Plate 17. The branch badge of crossed rifles appears on the collar outside the national insignia. Rank is indicated only by the badge pinned to the outer end of the shoulder straps – in this case the two silver bars of a Captain. The tunic is otherwise undecorated. It has four large patch pockets fastened with bronze buttons, which also appear down the front of the tunic and on the shoulders. The breeches are pegged, and lace from ankle to knee. Cross-strapped leather leggings and laced shoes are worn; like the belt and holster, these are now in 'russet' leather, not black. A .38 revolver and a sword are worn with service dress. This officer is examining one of the razor-edged chopping knives used by the Moro headhunters, whose activities caused the occupation forces great difficulty in the early years of the century.

Militia units which served in the tropics in the Spanish-American War and its immediate aftermath wore various collar insignia on this uniform. Some retained State insignia on the collar, together with regimental numbers; others adopted the 'USV' cypher.

76. Private of US Infantry, tropical service dress, 1903
This soldier wears the enlisted man's version of the 1898 khaki uniform. It should be pointed out that he would rarely wear the haversack, canteen and blanket roll in conjunction with service, as opposed to campaign dress; they have been included for completeness.

The uniform is simple and neat. The only insignia worn are the regimental number and company letter pinned to the crown of the campaign hat in bronze finish metal, the cords in the branch colour (this was a period when white and pale blue were used side by side owing to rapidly countermanded orders and the existence of stocks of both) and the national cypher and crossed rifle branch badge on the collar. The uniform is very similar to that of the officer in cut. The Krag rifle and Mills cartridge belt are still the main equipment throughout the army.

On campaign the most usual dress was still the blue shirt and khaki trousers, and an old campaign hat without badge or cords. Officially the crease in the crown of the hat gave way to the four-dimple 'Montana' style in 1912, but such esoteric instructions took a long time to filter through to troops in the overseas zones.

Illustrations exist which suggest that, in the cavalry at least, the khaki service dress was enlivened by distinctions in the branch colour. These seem to take the form of plain shoulder straps in the branch colour for non-commissioned ranks; and coloured stand-up collars, cuffs, and shoulder 'boxes' attached to the shoulder straps for officers. It seems probable that in this, too, standardisation of uniform and insignia practice was very imperfect in the years between 1898 and 1908-1910.

77. Sergeant of US Infantry, parade dress, 1905
This non-commissioned officer wears the last suit of 'blues' issued to the army as a whole for parade wear, which appeared in 1902. It neatly illustrates the confusion between light blue and white as a branch colour for the infantry. The stand-up collar, shoulder straps, cuffs and decorative cords of the tunic are in light blue, the chevrons and trouser stripes in white. In, say, the cavalry, all these items would be in yellow, as would the two bands around the stiff cap.

The chevrons are of the new small, reversed pattern officially introduced in 1902; stocks of the old style were often worn, reversed, while they lasted, at least on the tropical service uniform. Drab-coloured chevrons for all branches were worn with the new 'olive drab' general service uniform which also appeared in that year.

The insignia of the branch, with regimental number and company letter, is worn in gilt metal on the crown of the stiff cap. It is repeated on each side of the stiff collar, together with the 'US' cypher. With parade dress the waist belt was the only harness worn; this NCO wears his new russet leather belt, but retains for the time being his black shoes, until it is necessary to replace them.

78. Corporal of US Marine Infantry, 1910
Yet another example of the transitional state of American uniforms in the years before the outbreak of World War I. The Marine Corps, which had seen service in the China expedition under Chaffee in 1900, in Cuba and in the Philippines, represented one of the few units of the forces consistently battle-ready throughout the last decade of the 19th Century and the first of the 20th. This corporal wears his old-fashioned dark blue tunic still, with the large red Marine chevrons reversed in a concession to the new regulations. For field service he wears the khaki drill trousers of the tropical uniform – he is dressed as he would be for travel in a climate such as China's – and the familiar canvas leggings and campaign hat, still creased fore-and-aft. It is distinguished by the famous globe, eagle and anchor badge of his corps pinned to the crown. His canteen cover, back pack and haversack are stencilled 'USMC'; the canteen is hitched to his belt rather than being slung around his body. The belt and suspenders are the new webbing issue, with ammunition pouches for the 1903 Springfield magazine rifle.

79. Mexican irregular cavalry, 1916
A 'Villista', a rider of Pancho Villa's guerilla forces which raided the United States and provoked the punitive expedition into Mexico led by Pershing. His dress is entirely civilian, and entirely to personal taste. The vast quantity of ammunition slung around his body is characteristic; a guerilla army can never be certain of supplies, and the wise guerilla carries off what he can, whenever he can!

80. Trooper of US Cavalry, 1916
Most of the troops led into the state of Chihuahua by Brigadier-General Pershing were, for obvious reasons of terrain and the nature of the enemy, mounted units. This trooper wears a simple and practical uniform for

desert columns. The tunic of his 1902
'olive drab' uniform has been discarded, and
he wears 'shirtsleeve order' with the breeches of
the normal general service uniform. The
cross-strapped leggings of the mounted soldier,
boots, and automatic pistol holster are of
russet leather. He wears the 'mounted' version
of the webbing ammunition belt, and carries his
Springfield rifle, and a saddle-bag. Apart
from the cavalry yellow cords, his campaign hat
is also distinguished by a pair of tinted goggles
which he has 'acquired' somehow. These were
not issue items, but were sometimes used,
usually by officers.

7 'Over There'

One of a series of photos taken at Tours in June 1918, for the US Army Equipment Board, showing an AEF infantryman in full equipment. The 'overseas cap' (actually issued overseas) is worn here with the olive drab service uniform, and 1902 webbing harness and pouches. Note the hilt of the bayonet visible over the left shoulder, and the use of puttees in place of canvas leggings. *Imperial War Museum*

In retrospect it is tempting to see the pause in American military activity (on any significant scale) between the end of the Spanish-American War and the entry into World War I as some kind of conscious 'girding of the loins'. Politically this is nonsense – isolationism was still an enormous force in the land. In the sense of historical inevitability, however, this period offers a text-book example of a nation at the crossroads.

America was tremendously strong in man-power, technology, and vigour, and that strength was growing as each day passed. She had begun to feel a real sense of identity in the world. Internal divisions and internal challenges had receded in the face of a growing nationalism. American troops now stood on foreign soil, and the Union had acquired overseas possessions – although these facts did not prevent Americans from indulging in the favourite sport of 'twisting the Lion's tail'.

The Guantanamo enclave was to remain US sovereign territory, as was Puerto Rico. The Panama Canal Zone was declared an American Protectorate in 1903. Haiti was occupied between 1914 and 1934, and the Dominican Republic between 1916 and 1924. Nicaragua was occupied intermittently between 1909 and 1939. All these territories required an active military presence, and provided frequent opportunities for officers and men to gain experience in 'police actions'.

The reforms which followed the Cuban campaign included a rationalisation of the age-old militia problem. From 1903 onwards the entire structure was known as the National Guard, drilled, equipped and trained along Regular lines by Regular officers, and with the obligation of up to nine months Federal service at a time. The National Defense Act of 1916 divided the forces into three sections: Regulars, Organised Reserves, and National

Rear view, showing the rolled coat and blanket, the canteen in its webbing pocket, and the steel helmet of British pattern and the spade strapped to the 'long pack'. This latter protruded so far down behind the wearer's buttocks that he could not sit comfortably on any flat surface; it hampered the soldier in action, tended to tip his helmet over his eyes, was of inflexible design and would not easily accommodate any item not specifically planned for during the design process, and was generally loathed by the troops. *Imperial War Museum*

Guard. The standing army was increased to 175,000.

On April 6th, 1917 President Wilson took America into World War I, and the passing of the Selective Service Act some six weeks later ensured that volunteers and draftees were taken into the forces at roughly the same rate. While this system worked well, there were still enormous difficulties involved in training, equipping and transporting the tens of thousands of young men who flooded into the new army, and who would eventually total more than 4,000,000. The Springfield rifle of 1903 was available for only 300,000 of them; some 1,100 machine guns were on hand, and about 400 field guns. There were no heavy guns, tanks, aircraft, grenades or trench mortars – and this army was to be sent into a war in which the European powers had reached a deadly efficiency with all the tools evolved over the last three years. Industry got into its stride quickly, but throughout America's involvement in the war her armies relied entirely on British and French equipment in many vital areas.

Eventually, commanded by General John J. Pershing, the American Expeditionary Force arrived in England and France; by the end of hostilities the United States had an army of more than 2,000,000 at the front. The clamour for the fresh American troops to fill gaps and weak spots in the exhausted Allied line was firmly resisted by Pershing. When the 'doughboys' finally went into action they would be fully trained, fully equipped, and serving under American command. When the blooding finally came, around Chateau-Thierry and Belleau Wood in late May and early June 1918, the AEF fulfilled its promise. It was a splendid young army, full of dash and courage, full of enthusiasm, and, above all, full of energy and confidence. The troops might be green, but they were still in that mood which finds the

Group of AEF hospital orderlies photographed 'horsing around' in France. The men on the left wear the lightweight cotton version of the olive drab service dress, those on the right the heavier serge version. Note the maroon and white hat cords of these medical personnel; and the caduceus device on the segeant's chevrons. The belts and boots are russet leather, the buckles plain brass frames, the collar discs dull bronze. The canvas leggings are of an early pattern. *Imperial War Museum*

Officers of the US 77th Division confer with a British staff officer. Note the variety of leg coverings; the cuff braid of commisioned rank; and the style of revolver holster worn by the Lieutenant on the left. His binocular case, haversack, mapcase, Sam Browne belt and webbing pistol belt contrive to produce a somewhat festooned appearance. Note the officers' collar insignia— the national cyphers worn well forward, and the arm of service badges worn back in line with the epaulettes. *Imperial War Museum*

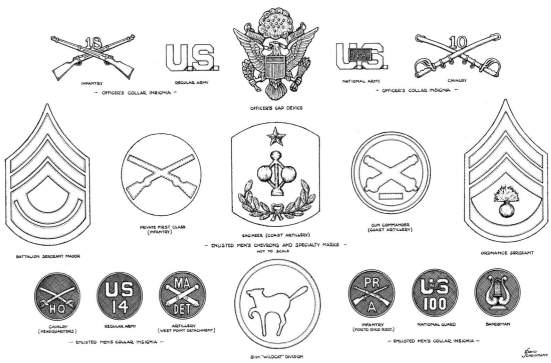

INFANTRY | REGULAR ARMY
— OFFICER'S COLLAR INSIGNIA —

OFFICER'S CAP DEVICE

NATIONAL ARMY | CAVALRY
— OFFICER'S COLLAR INSIGNIA —

BATTALION SERGEANT MAJOR

PRIVATE FIRST CLASS
(INFANTRY)

ENGINEER (COAST ARTILLERY)

GUN COMMANDER
(COAST ARTILLERY)

ORDNANCE SERGEANT

— ENLISTED MEN'S CHEVRONS AND SPECIALTY MARKS —
NOT TO SCALE

CAVALRY
(HEADQUARTERS)

REGULAR ARMY

ARTILLERY
(WEST POINT DETACHMENT)

— ENLISTED MEN'S COLLAR INSIGNIA —

81ST. "WILDCAT" DIVISION

INFANTRY
(PORTO RICO REGT.)

NATIONAL GUARD

BANDSMAN

— ENLISTED MEN'S COLLAR INSIGNIA —

TYPES OF FIRST WORLD WAR INSIGNIA AND RANK MARKINGS

possibility of defeat inconceivable. The Tommies and *poilus*, infinitely more experienced, more crafty, more schooled in the special disciplines and tricks of modern war, were also infinitely more tired. They had been in Hell for nearly four years, and had very nearly reached the end of their strength. They watched in wonderment as the endless regiments of naive, cocky, brawny young soldiers swelled the American sectors, bursting with a fine arrogance which had not been seen in the British and French lines since 1914. In January 1918 the AEF held six miles of front, against 462 miles held by the British, French and Belgians. In March the AEF had 162,000 men at the front. In August they had ninety miles of front. In September they had a million men. In October they held 101 miles of front. Their infantry divisions had an establishment of about 25,000 men, their companies, 250 men; about twice the strength of British, French or German units.

By November the German leaders could see quite plainly that the entire structure of their forces, and their nation, was cracking under the pressure; rather than wait for inevitable total collapse, they sued for peace. The AEF, less 48,000 battle dead and 62,000 dead of influenza, went home. Too much Home Front rhetoric about how America had got in there with Yankee know-how and won the war the Europeans had been fouling up caused a stupid and needless resentment between nations who had stood together in battle; but the blame for this can hardly be laid at the door of the military men, who could readily appreciate the difference between America's six months in the firing line, and 48,000 deaths,

The M1917 steel helmet of British design, worn here with the British pattern gasmask and the cotton service dress.

and Britain's four and a half years, and 765,000 deaths.

In the years between the World Wars the military stature of America suffered from a tide of isolationist and anti-war feeling. Just as in Europe the shocked and exhausted victors turned in revulsion from any faint thought that they might have to fight again in the foreseeable future, so in America it became electoral suicide to agitate for money to be spent on military preparedness rather than on the very real domestic problems. The sordid political history of Europe between 1919 and 1939 seemed to argue that American intervention and sacrifice had been in vain, and 'America First' became the ruling sentiment.

Despite this mood, and despite the danger to any officer's career of making too much noise about military expenditure, there was not a total retreat from reality. By 1925 the army had been cut back to 136,000 men, but those areas which World War I experience had shown to be deficient were gradually improved. A programme of research and development saw the manufacture of the first indigenous tanks – militarily insignificant, but a start. A military aircraft industry was born, and as the years passed it produced some excellent designs. The horse cavalry was marked for extinction – a fate it met as stubbornly and with as much obtuse and sentimental argument as in every other country – and the foundations were being laid for great advances in artillery techniques. Although a buck private was only paid $18:00 per month – just two dollars more than his grandfather, who rode with Custer! – the skeleton upon which a realistic wartime army might be rebuilt was kept in being. The two-fold weakness of an army starved of funds between wars was to have its inevitable price in 1941 and 1942, however.

An army in reduced circumstances must spend a disproportionate amount on 'running expenses', and has little to spare for the development of modern weapons. Industry, starved of Government projects, devotes its research bureaux and production lines to consumer goods. When military equipment of up-to-date design is needed in a hurry, not only are the aircraft and guns not available, but neither are the men to design them or the machines to build them. In launching a modern nation into war, the existence of a hard core of experienced men in industry is just as important as the availability of drill sergeants in reception camps.

In the event, America had a little time in which to prepare herself for global war. On September 16th, 1940, prodded by a President who was convinced that for her own sake America must support the Allies, a Congress alarmed by the fall of France and the desperate defence of Britain passed the Compulsory Military Service Act, giving the United States an army of one and a half million. While the nation moved towards open commitment by slow footsteps – Lend-Lease in March 1941, the occupation of Greenland and Iceland in the summer, the widening of the sphere of naval activity in the Atlantic – the industrial machine began it metamorphosis. There was a very powerful isolationist lobby, with great popular support, in the Mid-West especially. It took more than arguments to change the mood of the people. When Mitsuo Fuchida

Interesting view of Negro enlisted men and white Lieutenant of the 369th Infantry, 93rd Division, in trenches at Maffrescourt on 5th May 1918. The men wear olive drab uniforms with French leather equipment and blue Adrian helmets; their weapons are the Lebel rifle of 1886 and the 'Chauchat' automatic rifle— an unreliable weapon, but the best available in large quantities before the arrival of the B.A.R. *Imperial War Museum*

looked down on 'Battleship Row' from the
cockpit of his Nakajima in the dawn of
December 7th, 1941, he was uniting the
American nation and throwing it into the
Allied cause with a commitment ten times more
complete than the speeches of Churchill and
Roosevelt had ever achieved.

In the Phillipines the small army of regulars
and native units, still partially equipped with
1918 vintage material and suddenly bereft of
the naval and air power around which their
defence had been planned, went down fighting.
Their example inspired the nation, and reinforced the hunger for revenge which Pearl
Harbour had awakened. The means for
revenge were at hand. An army of three
million men was available in 1942, an army
assembled, sorted, trained, equipped and
formed into units with almost total efficiency;
mobilisation went smoothly through all its
phases. At its peak, the US Army in World
War II would comprise 12,300,000 men.
From inadequate and mismanaged beginnings,
the war effort would grow in the space of three
years into the greatest military machine any
nation had ever fielded in recorded history.

Alone of the combatants, America had unlimited industrial capacity, unlimited money,
unlimited food and raw materials, and un-
disturbed immunity from enemy attack. No
American factory worker ever came on shift
red-eyed and tense from a night in an air-raid
shelter amid the sounds and sights of his home-
town being smashed flat. No American community ever trudged the endless roads with
their salvaged possessions on their backs, in
terror of strafing fighters. No American
soldier returned to his home on leave to find
the streets and squares where he had played
as a child turned into a bewildering maze of
rubble. From this secure base America sent
her men and her machinery to battlefields in

US Airborne troops in Normandy, June 1944. They wear a mixture of paratroop jump-suits and normal infantry field jackets. Note the details of webbing equipment; the airborne shoulder patch; the censored divisional shoulder patches; the chin cup on the paratrooper's helmet (third from left); and the Garand M1 rifle in the foreground. *Imperial War Museum*

The famous and much-exported M1 steel helmet, with its fibre liner and a reversible camouflage-printed cover. The steel shell's matt finish is produced by mixing sand with the last coat of paint.

3rd Armored Division crews with their Sherman tanks, somewhere in Europe during the winter of 1944-45. Note the padded tank helmet, the zipped field jacket worn over the bulky tank-suit, and the metal-clipped storm boots. *Imperial War Museum*

Webbing pistol belt, with russet leather holster for the .45 automatic, small first aid pouch, and spare clip pouches. This has been the favoured sidearm of the **US** soldier since World War I. *Max Sarche*

All **US** armored divisions wore the same design of shoulder patch, a yellow, red and blue triangle with a black central device crossed by a red lightning bolt, with the divisional number in black.

the South Pacific, Burma, Italy, North Africa, and continental Europe. Although her sacrifice in manpower was slightly less than that of the British Commonwealth, her apparently inexhaustible strength was, beyond all doubt, the deciding factor in the war. Once committed, America simply overwhelmed every army and every geographical obstacle which stood in her way.

Twenty years before the American soldier had to wear a helmet copied from the British, fire a machine-gun bought from the French, and travel to battle in foreign ships; ahead of him the wire was crushed by British tanks, and above him his countrymen flew French aircraft. In World War II the Allied armies drew on the products of American industry and wealth. The Sherman tank was driven into action by men of a dozen nations, the Mustang fighter bore the markings of every Allied air arm, and soldiers in the uniforms of every country under arms against the Axis rode American trucks and half-tracks, carried American automatic weapons, ate American rations, and were saved by American drugs. The range of carefully designed clothing and equipment which America lavished on her soldiers was the envy of the world; and the expertise of all supporting and servicing arms of the US forces speeded the advance of the Allies on every front. The numbers were staggering. More than 88,000 tanks: 63,000 field guns: 66,000 fighters and 34,000 bombers: more than 328 million shells: nearly a million machine-guns, excluding aircraft and anti-aircraft weapons: nearly three million trucks. Whole new sciences – amphibious warfare, and the harnessing of nuclear power, to name but two – were perfected. In every nation the years of World War II produced enormous technical advances, and as the technical capital of the world America advanced further than most.

The soldier himself has been studied and analysed to the point of tedium, and when all is said and done there was little new about him. He was healthy, well fed, and physically impressive. He was basically cynical, but responded to appeals to his sense of fairness, responsibility, and personal or unit pride. He was not particularly well disciplined, but this led to few problems in the front line – battle produces its own discipline. He was capable of great dash and enjoyed the flamboyant gesture. He regarded all senior officers with a thoroughly healthy scepticism. He learned very quickly from past mistakes, and when tempered by battlefield experience proved as determined, crafty, and dangerous a soldier as any country could wish.

PLATES 17, 18, 19

81. Sergeant of US Artillery, 1917

This NCO wears the standard issue 1902 olive drab uniform worn as service and field dress by the American Expeditionary Force. The artillery scarlet cords on his campaign hat (later almost universally discarded in favour of the 'overseas cap') distinguish his branch; other major branch colours were scarlet and white mixed (engineers), orange and white mixed (signals), maroon and white mixed (medical), and buff (quartermaster personnel). Officers of all branches wore gold and black cords, and generals gold cords.

On the stand-up collar of the tunic appear two round bronze badges embossed with the national cypher (right) and the branch of service device and unit number (left) – in this case the crossed cannons and battery letter. In 1907/08 these disc badges were introduced for enlisted men, officers reverting simultaneously to the cut-out national cyphers worn earlier. At first the men wore two discs on each side, both the national cypher and branch badges appearing on left and right. After about 1912 they were worn singly, a cypher badge on the right and a branch badge with regimental number and company or battery letter on the left. Again, in 1918, the style was changed to that of wearing the national cypher with the regimental number on the right, and the branch badge with the company letter on the left. The variations were probably worn side by side throughout the AEF in France. The only other insignia worn are the chevrons of a sergeant, point uppermost on each arm.

Conventional canvas webbing equipment is worn; the belt, with the russet leather holster for John Moses Browning's famous 1911 Government Model automatic and two webbing magazine pouches, is supported by suspenders which unite with the straps of the dreaded 1910 Model 'long pack'. A webbing bag slung on the chest contains the British-style gasmask of the period. The webbing leggings illustrated are a very early pattern, soon superceded. The whole appearance of this NCO is of a man 'just off the boat'.

82. Private of Infantry, 4th Division, 1918

The typical 'doughboy', as he appeared in the battles round the St Mihiel Salient in September 1918. His British pattern steel helmet has the green ivy leaf badge of his division stencilled on the front; apart from his collar badges this is the only insignia worn in action. Divisional shoulder devices were worn in 1918, but rarely if ever in combat.

This soldier is hung about with his full field equipment. The 'long pack' is worn, complete with greatcoat and blanket lashed around it in a horseshoe roll. The webbing belt carries ten pouches for rifle ammunition; they are designed to accommodate eight-round clips for the 1903 Springfield .30 calibre weapon illustrated here. (The .03 Springfield was one of many items in short supply when America entered World War I. Winchester and Remington production lines, already turning out Enfield-designed rifles for the British Army, adapted the weapons to take the US cartridge; the resulting 'P.17', heavy and clumsy but reliable, was much used by American forces. It was still in limited service in the early stages of World War II, and was exported to Britain.) Extra bandoliers of cloth clip pouches are slung diagonally across the chest and ribs. Cloth-covered water canteens, small webbing pouches for first aid kits, and webbing bags for gasmasks, grenades, and other extra equipment were all carried on the belt or slung in some convenient place on the body; one of the faults of the 1910 pack was that it did not provide convenient stowage for items not specifically considered when it was originally designed.

This soldier has a pair of wire-cutters strung to his belt, and a trench knife with a knuckle-duster hilt thrust in its sheath into the top of his leggings, ready to hand. These leggings, with extensions to cover the laced aperture of the boot, straps passing under the instep, and hook-and-lace fastening all the way up the outside seam, were a later issue than those shown in the previous illustration; they, too, presented supply problems, and delays in production of sufficient stocks frequently led to the adoption of cloth puttees – leg-bandages – in the style favoured by the British and French. Finally it may be mentioned that the scabbard for the bayonet was not worn on the belt, as in other armies of the day, but was fitted to the pack, so that the bayonet could be drawn over the left shoulder. It would normally be moved down to the belt when – as frequently happened under field conditions – the full pack was left off and the necessary minimum of kit was carried wrapped in a horseshoe blanket roll around the body.

83. Captain of US Infantry, 1918

This officer wears the normal field kit for-commissioned ranks, with the exception of the steel helmet. Here he wears the jaunty and practical side-cap or 'overseas cap', piped around the edge of the flap in his branch of service colour – infantry light blue; a rank badge is pinned to the left side, well forward.

Insignia on the stand-up collar comprise bronze cut-out 'US' cyphers nearest the join of the collar, and cut-out branch of service badges in the usual style – here, the crossed rifles and a unit number. On the outer end of the shoulder straps are pinned his rank insignia, the two bars of a Captain. Commissioned rank is also indicated by the strip of brown braid around the cuff of the tunic.

There tended to be considerable variation in the details of cut and shade of officer's tunics, due both to individual taste and to the practice of having uniforms tailored in Britain and France, widespread among Pershing's officers. The leather 'Sam Browne' belt was another feature copied by AEF officers from their British counterparts; it is worn here, under the webbing pistol belt of US issue, which carries the usual leather holster and webbing pouches for the .45 automatic. (Revolvers were sometimes carried as sidearms in place of the automatic; .45 calibre Colt and Smith & Wesson models were both favoured) The webbing gasmask bag is slung over the right shoulder and hangs on the left hip. The leather strap over the left shoulder supports the binocular case, often pushed round to the back for comfort. The cross-strapped leather leggings worn over laced ankle boots are characteristic of this period; they offered a better combination of comfort, protection and flexibility than the prescribed knee-boots.

84. Brigadier-General, AEF Staff, 1918

This 'One-Star General' on Pershing's staff wears the usual officer's tunic and breeches, and the lack of encumbrances allows a better view of the close similarity between the uniforms of officers and enlisted men, in points of cut, if not of quality.

The officer's service cap is worn, olive drab in shade, with brown leather peak and chinstrap and the bronze finish national badge first adopted at the turn of the century. The tunic collar bears the national cypher, and the branch emblem of the staff, a five-pointed star with the national badge superimposed. The single silver star of Brigadier-General's rank is pinned to the shoulder straps. General rank is also indicated by the strip of black braid around the tunic cuffs. The tunic buttons are of bronze finish. The prescribed brown riding boots are worn, and this officer is one of the many who favour the wearing of spurs – either for practical reasons, or vanity!

85. Private, 369th Infantry Regiment, 1918

The majority of Negro units in the AEF were confined to the labour and service rôle, due to prevailing social attitudes which it would serve no purpose to discuss here at greater length; suffice it to say that the combat record of the 369th, 370th, 371st and 372nd Infantry gave the lie to them. Renumbered in March 1918 from the Harlem-based 15th New York Infantry of the National Guard, the 369th went into action the following month. It fought on the Champagne front, in the Vosges, and was reputed to be the first Allied unit to actually reach the banks of the Rhine. The regiment was under fire for 191 days, longer than any other US unit; it never lost a prisoner, but suffered about 1,500 combat casualties including 367 dead.

The four Negro infantry regiments which made up the main strength of the 93rd Infantry Division of the AEF never served together as a single formation, but were employed separately alongside various French units – thus the French equipment, the horizon blue French Adrian steel helmet, the Lebel rifle, and the divisional emblem of a stylised Adrian helmet in pale blue on a black disc. The basic uniform is the standard AEF olive drab issue, with the usual collar badges in bronze. Puttees are worn around the legs, in the French fashion. The Adrian helmet, complete with the embossed grenade badge and horizon blue paint, came straight from French stocks and displays no national alterations or insignia. The black leather belt and Y-straps support three leather cartridge pouches, two on the front and one worn centrally at the back. An ochre-coloured canvas haversack or *musette* is slung on the left hip, and the French canteen or *bidon,* covered in dark blue cloth, hangs on the right hip from a diagonal leather strap. The 1886 Lebel 8mm rifle, with an eight-round tubular magazine, is the standard French infantry issue, as is the 20-inch needle bayonet with its smooth white metal grip.

86. Corporal of US Infantry, 1942

The service uniform of World War I was replaced in 1926 by a rig which featured an open collar exposing a shirt and black tie, a peaked service cap for all ranks, and leather leggings replacing cloth puttees for all ranks; the pegged breeches were retained. By the late 1930s these latter had been replaced by trousers, restricted in combat by canvas spat-type gaiters of almost identical design to those worn in 1918. The peaked service cap, the overseas cap and the old campaign hat were all worn with various dress orders, in various seasonal weights. In 1941 there was a breakthrough in uniform design. The olive drab service tunic was relegated to full dress and walking out, and a field jacket was issued for working and combat dress, in conjunction with the olive drab trousers. This was a windcheater-style garment in olive drab cotton fabric, with buttoning cuff-bands and slanted, flapless chest pockets. At first very popular, it was found to have drawbacks due to the particular materials used.

Summer combat dress consisted of the olive drab trousers, the olive flannel shirt worn without a tie, and webbing gaiters and field equipment. Tropical service and combat dress was as illustrated – a very pale, lightweight twill shirt and trousers, which could be worn either with or without a tie of the same material, worn tucked between the second and third shirt buttons. (The black tie of temperate zone service dress changed to olive drab in February 1942.) The normal headgear with this outfit would be the lightweight tropical overseas cap.

In the early fighting in the Philippines the American soldier still wore the British-style steel helmet and the webbing equipment of the 1920s. Rank insignia would normally be the only badges worn on the uniform in the presence of the enemy. This NCO carries a Browning Automatic Rifle, the sturdy and attractive .30 calibre light automatic support weapon which saw service, in a succession of versions, from 1918 well into the 1950s. His webbing harness is augmented by a waistbelt of large pouches carrying spare 20-round box magazines for the BAR. Although it had many fine qualities, the BAR was still inferior to contemporary foreign equipment in the sense that it was not capable of providing the infantry squad with a useful rate of sustained fully automatic fire, as could the British Bren, the German MG.34 and MG.42, the French FM 24/29 or the Russian Degtyarev. Considering the generally dominant position enjoyed by America in many areas of military design, this gap in the US Army's arsenal is puzzling.

87. Lieutenant of Infantry, 3rd Division, European theatre, 1944

In vivid contrast to the previous figure, this platoon commander in field dress and combat equipment reflects the attitudes of the mid-war years. No longer reliant on foreign experience and last-war philosophies, the American army profited by hard combat experience to produce a wide range of extremely practical uniform items, geared to the realities of the battlefield.

The British-style helmet has been replaced (since 1942) by the universally famous M1 style, used ever since by the forces of the USA and many other nations. It consists of a steel outer shell to which the chinstrap is attached, and a plasticised fibre composition inner shell or 'liner'. Thus the light liner can be worn alone when behind the line, rather than the heavy and more tiring steel shell. The outer shell can be used as a seat, a wash-basin, even a soup kettle or entrenching tool in emergencies, and then worn immediately without thorough cleaning. The liner can be painted or chromed for ceremonial purposes, without destroying the usefulness of the helmet as combat wear. Rank devices were often painted on the helmets, as here, for quick identification in combat.

With his service uniform trousers of olive drab wool – actually a dark brown shade – the lieutenant wears the M43 field jacket. This was made of proofed material of a greenish shade, wind and water repellent; trousers of the same material were also issued, but the combination illustrated here was often observed. (The 3rd Division were the first unit to test the new outfit in action, at Anzio in 1943.) Various pile liners, woollen sweaters, and so forth, were worn under the basic field uniform depending on weather conditions. Knitted woollen stocking caps or toques were often worn under the steel helmet. This officer wears one of several late-war styles of combat boot – a design combining a high-lacing boot with a buckled ankle-flap which acted as a built-in gaiter. A minimum of equipment is carried in combat. This officer does not wear the usual leather holster for the .45 calibre automatic on his webbing pistol belt, but only his canteen and a first aid pouch, and spare magazine pouches for his .30 calibre M1 carbine. A leather map case is slung on a diagonal strap; the officer's bars of rank are pinned to the shoulder straps of his field jacket, and the divisional emblem is sewn to the left shoulder.

The excellent M1 carbine largely replaced the

sidearm as the weapon of officers and other junior leaders. Its self-loading action and 15-round box magazine gave it a useful rate of rapid fire; it is still an extremely popular weapon all over the world. Spare magazines are carried, here, in pouches clipped around the butt of the carbine itself. Skeleton and folding-butt versions were also issued.

88. US Marine Raider, Pacific theatre, 1943
Impressed by the results achieved by British Commando units in raids on enemy-occupied Europe, the United States Marine Corps formed its first two Raider Battalions in 1942. They carried out several daring operations against Japanese-held islands in the Pacific, and an expanded Raider force went on to fight in a more conventional role on Guadalcanal and New Georgia. The Raiders were re-absorbed into the Marine Infantry regiments when the need for their special type of operation disappeared.

This rifleman wears the M1 steel helmet, with the addition of a camouflage-printed cover. Several different styles of cloth helmet cover were issued in the various theatres of operations, ranging from specially patterned seasonal camouflage to simple drab-coloured cloth which merely killed all reflections and could be camouflaged to taste with mud and foliage. His uniform is the camouflage-printed two piece jungle suit in herringbone twill which replaced the earlier one-piece suit at the turn of 1942-43; one-piece suits had certain practical disadvantages in the field, which should be obvious to the reader after a moment's thought ... By late 1944 the camouflage pattern had been discarded in favour of simple olive drab, although it is interesting to note that at one point during the battles in Normandy in the summer of 1944 camouflage suits were requested by, and issued to, units fighting in close country. In 1945 a simple green poplin jungle uniform in two parts replaced all other styles still in use in the Pacific theatre. This Raider has the initials of his corps and the eagle, globe and anchor insignia stencilled in black ink on the chest of his jacket. The trousers hang free over the boots, although canvas gaiters were still official issue to most troops at this time; the boots are of leather, and were replaced later in the war by special canvas and rubber jungle boots. A minimum of equipment is carried for patrol or raiding operations – this soldier wears only sufficient webbing to carry his ammunition, bayonet and

water. The rifle is the outstanding M1 Garand .30 calibre self-loading weapon, the GI's standard issue weapon throughout the war and for years afterwards.

89. US Parachute Infantryman, European theatre, 1944
The special rôle, and special handicaps, of airborne troops have tended to ensure that paratroopers have been regarded as élite soldiers, the world over. America is no exception. Duly noting the achievements of Germany's large and active airborne arm in the early war years, America formed her own two famous airborne divisions – the 82nd, and 101st 'Screaming Eagles' – in 1942.

The paratrooper illustrated wears the M1 helmet covered with green string netting for the attachment of foliage. The helmet also has a special double chinstrap with a rubber chin-cup, to hold it secure during the jump. For ease of access he has attached his first aid package to his helmet netting. His field jacket and trousers are of a special design. They have capacious pockets, and patches of reinforcement at knee and elbow; and the breast pockets are tilted, to make access easier when buckled and cinched into the paratrooper's bulky equipment. The greyish green shade of these airborne field uniforms, dangerously close to 'field grey', prompted the issue of the unique national flag shoulder patch worn by this type of unit on the right shoulder. On the left shoulder it was balanced by the divisional badge – either the 82nd's two white As on a blue disc on a red square, or the white eagle's head on a black shield of the 101st. The high-lacing jump-boots were for some time a proud mark of distinction, peculiar to this arm of service, but the distinction disappeared with the later issue of high-lacing combat boots to all US troops. Webbing equipment is bulky and complex – the airborne soldier carries all his necessities on his back, or slung around him in musette bags. It includes such conventional items as knapsack and pouches, reversed entrenching tool, and so forth; fighting knives were carried strapped to the leg. This paratrooper carries the M3 'Grease Gun' – so called in allusion to its shape – which was developed in order to fill the need for a light, simple, cheap submachine gun comparable to the British Sten and the German MP.40. Initially two of these .45 calibre weapons were issued to each infantry squad; they proved to be a great deal more convenient to handle in

action than the heavy Thompson gun of similar calibre.

90. Technical Sergeant, 2nd Armored Division, European theatre, 1945
Another example of the specialised clothing produced in such variety for the US forces. This tank commander wears a padded, ventilated crash-helmet with built-in earphone housings, issued to all US tank units and since exported widely. He wears a one-piece olive drab twill tank-suit, and over it a simple and practical windcheater jacket of proofed material with slanting pockets, a zip front, and knitted collar, cuffs and waistband. His boots are a late issue; lacking the buckled flap, they closely resemble paratroop issue.

The insignia of this NCO's rank – the three chevrons and two 'rockers' of a Technical Sergeant, in the usual light drab on dark blue – appear on each upper arm. On his left shoulder is his divisional patch, a universal design adopted by all Armored Divisions, varying only in the numeral in the upper, yellow segment. The personal sidearm is the usual .45 calibre automatic, worn in a leather holster on a webbing belt; the only other equipment carried on the person are the webbing pistol magazine pouches and the small first aid kit.

91. Brigadier-General, 1st Infantry Division, European theatre, 1945
It should be pointed out immediately that this illustration is not intended to be a portrait of the commander of the famous 'Bloody One', but is simply a representative composite!

This general wears the overseas cap, piped in gold around the edge of the flap to indicate general officer's rank, and bearing the single silver star of this exact rank pinned to the left side, well forward. His shirt and tie are pale in shade – 'olive drab' is a phrase which covers as wide a spectrum as 'khaki', and in an army indulgent of personal taste who has more freedom than a general? The short, fly-fronted 'Ike jacket' was introduced in 1944; it was a copy of the British battledress blouse, which much impressed the Americans, although their development of the idea was a great deal smarter and of superior material. It was issued to all ranks and branches, and was intended for use as a field jacket. In practice, however, the GI usually saved it for wearing on leave – the average 'dogface' was properly conscious of the figure he cut in public, and considered the blouse was too smart to waste in muddy foxholes.

On the collar is the cut-out 'US' cypher in gilt metal. Silver rank stars are pinned to the shoulder straps, and the divisional patch – the famous 'Bloody One' on a bronze shield – is sewn to the left shoulder. Campaign and gallantry decoration ribbons are worn on the breast, as is the silver and blue Combat Infantry badge; this was only awarded to colonels and below, and thus indicates that this general held a junior front-line command earlier in the war. The .45 calibre automatic is worn in a leather shoulder rig of a type popular with American generals. The boots are of one of several foul weather designs issued, in this case rubberised fabric storm-boots with four metal clip fasteners on the front.

PLATE 17

81

82

83

84

85

PLATE 18

86

88

89

87

90

8 The World's Policeman

The quarter-century since the close of the Second World War has seen American troops committed to two major wars overseas, and a number of minor involvements in areas of the world susceptible to the current disease of 'brushfire war'. As the richest and most heavily committed member of the newly formed United Nations Organisation – and as one of those members who actually pay their agreed contributions – America consciously took on the role of the world's policeman. A genuine attachment to the ideals of democracy, and an unwillingness to see smaller nations subverted or openly invaded by totalitarian powers, combined with other motives to set America on the course of actively exercised world power.

A large part of the US forces under arms was committed to occupation duty in Germany and Japan immediately the shooting stopped. The questionable joys of occupation were not to last for long, however; in 1950 the Communists invaded South Korea, and a startled, unready army was thrown into the line to stop them. The Korean War set the pattern for future international crises; the other free nations expressed horror and despatched what troops they could spare, while America carried the major burden of fighting the war. This pattern was inevitable, bearing in mind the fact that of the Allies only America had come out of World War II domestically unscathed. The European powers had spent their treasure, and their young men, too lavishly; they had survived, they had won, but they were enfeebled for a generation. Only America was in any position to mount major operations so soon, and so regularly.

The GI in Korea was dressed and equipped in very much the same fashion as his comrades had been five years before. Although it had now been generally accepted that it was impractical to fight wearing a woollen uniform tunic and trousers designed for smartness rather than frontline convenience, and well designed combat clothing of proofed material was universally worn in action, the GI still found that the Brasshats were no match for the weather. The experience of what a Korean winter could do to infantry forced the development of really first class weatherproof clothing, which was available before the end of the fighting. The personal equipment used in Korea was generally satisfactory, but as always, combat pointed up small details which needed improvement. A reappraisal of exactly what the infantryman needed to carry on his back, coinciding in the mid-1950s with the relegation of the Garand rifle and the introduction of small arms which were unsuitably served by the old 1938 Model cartridge clip pouches, led to a new issue of webbing equipment in the late years of that decade. The process of reappraisal has continued ever since. Advances in weaponry and tactical concepts have made it necessary for the responsible authorities to 'tinker' ceaselessly with the infantryman's equipment, and such a vast number of specialised items of equipment and harness have appeared in the last twenty years that few generalisations are possible. Suffice it to say that the emphasis is firmly on lightness, convenience and flexibility of use under combat conditions.

Combat clothing has gone through the same continuous process of change. Though the goal of simplicity has been achieved, the number of special requirements has led to a proliferation of items and combinations worthy of earlier centuries. It should be firmly stated, however, that in quality the US Army's equipment is still outstanding. Special terrain clothing has reached a high peak of efficiency, Arctic and jungle dress alike. New materials which provide much improved insulation are

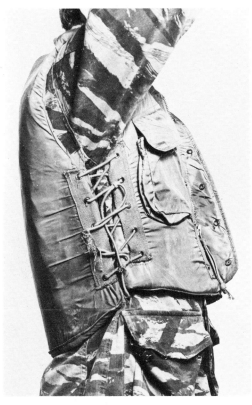

used, and for tropical wear a new pattern of fatigue and field dress has been evolved which, if it cannot repel the perpetual damp of the jungle, at least dries out more quickly than conventional drill clothing. Such small but important details as the siting of pockets so that they can be reached easily by a man wearing full equipment have been considered; readers with military experience may well feel that such attention to the comfort of the soldier is almost too sensible ever to have been thought out by a general!

The longdrawn and tragic war in Vietnam, politically controversial and the subject of much bitter feeling at home and abroad, has also produced far-reaching changes in the equipment of the soldier. New weapons and new tactics have emerged. The widespread use of camouflage clothing is a feature of the campaigns in South East Asia, as is the rein-

troduction of personal armour, in the form of splinterproof 'flak jackets' first used in the Korean War. Not very effective as a defence against modern military small arms, the jackets at least cut down casualties from shell and grenade fragments. This is an item of dress which has been adopted by the British Army as well in recent years, and it has proved itself in the 'operations in support of the civil power' which have been such a depressing feature of Western military experience during the 1960s. An item which has generally disappeared from the soldier's locker in recent years is the webbing legging or gaiter; again, other nations have followed the lead of the US Army in replacing this tedious piece of equipment with high-lacing combat boots of various designs.

The late 1950s also saw the introduction of the service uniform which has remained in use

151

The yellow and black divisional patch of the 1st Cavalry (Air).

Two versions of the 9th Division patch. *Top* is the normal red, white and blue patch on a silver cloth disc. *Bottom* is the 'subdued' version for wear on combat dress, as issued in Vietnam; it is made in olive drab and black for low visibility.

Often troops in the field mark this type of insignia directly on to combat clothing with marking pens or felt-writers rather than attaching patches to the jungle denims, which wear out very quickly in the damp weather.

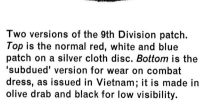

up to the present day. Khaki brown disappeared, and a smart new single-breasted tunic and trousers of dark green came into use. A round peaked cap of the same colour is worn with this uniform, which is identical in cut for officers and men. A pale tan shirt and a black tie complete the uniform, and leather items – cap peaks, chinstraps, shoes – are now black, in place of the russet brown which was in use from the time of the Spanish-American War.

Perhaps the most noticeable trend in the insignia of the US Army over the last two decades is the enormous proliferation of specialist ranks, grades, trades and units. Reflecting the complexity and sophistication of the forces in a nuclear age, these new ratings are frankly confusing to anyone but a born bureaucrat. The forces of other nations, just as technically advanced, have managed to maintain their efficiency alongside the time-honoured ranks; one wonders why America found it necessary to transform corporals and sergeants into 'Sp.3s' and 'E8s'.

Another feature of American uniforms has been the increasing attention paid to formal and full dress wear. The service uniform is smartened up for formal parades by the addition of coloured neckerchieves, braided shoulder cords, white gloves and polished combat boots. Such special cases as the 'buff strap' and Sam Browne belt of the US 3rd Infantry (see **96**, Plate 20) seem to point to a conscious effort to commemmorate the traditions of a proud military past. This admirable trait provides a thread of continuity in an Army which, to European eyes at least, is depressingly dominated by unit designations composed of huge and anonymous numbers. This is one, but not the only sign that the Pentagon has recognised the value to morale of a continuous regimental tradition, arguably one of the main strengths of British and European formations. It is only in relatively recent years that period uniforms and banners covered with battle honours have begun to figure largely in American military ceremonial, bringing the US Army, once more, into line with European custom.

In the mid-1950s a new full dress uniform for the Army appeared, recalling the blue and gold of Grant's day. It is usually, but by no means exclusively, observed as officer's wear, and is illustrated as **97,** Plate 20.

Finally, one should perhaps mention the foundation of the US Special Forces. This was originally a clandestine formation whose operations were closely bound up with the foreign policy objectives of the Central Intelligence Agency. (Men of the SF have carried out operations behind the Iron Curtain on several occasions, and small units fought in Budapest in support of the Hungarian uprising of 1956). In recent years, however, this CIA 'private army' has adopted a more open policy and has operated in a slightly more conventional way alongside the regular branches of the Army. Their uniform reflects several new features for the US Army, notably, of course, the famous green beret. To the present writer's knowledge the only previous unit to wear the beret was the bi-national Canadian-American Special Service Force raised by Colonel Frederick and employed in Italy during World War II; this unit was issued flame red berets. Some of their traditions are maintained by the Special Forces; the arrowhead shape of the shoulder patch, for instance, and the crossed arrows featured in the unit insignia. The Special Forces are also distinguished by the use of a unit cap badge (worn by non-commissioned personnel) in place of the previously

The dark green enlisted men's service cap, with black strap and peak and gilt buttons and national insignia. It is worn here with the open neck shirt of the 'Summer Class A' dress order. The collar brasses bear the national insignia of 'unassigned' troops. *Katcher*

universal national cap device; again, the formation is unique in wearing this unit device pinned to the shoulder straps.

In these trends, then, the United States Army appears to be coming closer to European practice in the fields of uniform and insignia. In view of the multi-national beginnings of this army, and the number of European countries which have played their part in the military history of North America, this can only seem fitting.

92. Private First Class, US Infantry, early 1950s

The infantry rifleman of the Korean War, little changed since the last months of World War II. The standard weapon is still the M1 Garand; the webbing harness is still built around the 1938 cartridge pouches, each holding an eight-round clip for the Garand; and the outer garments are still the familiar greenish proofed field jacket and trousers, worn over a variety of liners and sweaters. Increased use is made of helmet markings of various sorts, for quick identification and night work. The back pack is the 1945 equipment, with the sleeping bag and bed-roll lashed round it in a horseshoe shape. The canteen is worn on the right hip, and the reversed entrenching tool in its webbing cover is fixed to the back of the pack. Grenades were often carried with the safety pin splayed and the 'spoon' slipped through a convenient D-ring in the shoulder harness. The combat boots lace high on the ankle, and are worn without leggings (although the Marine infantryman of the period still wore the familiar canvas spats). The only insignia is the single reversed chevron of Pfc. rank, on both upper arms. Divisional insignia was worn or discarded according to the requirements of security.

As a result of experience in Korea, webbing equipment underwent several changes in the mid-1950s. The cartridge pouch belt was discarded in favour of two large universal pouches which can accommodate the various clips and magazines for a number of the newer infantry weapons. The horseshoe bed-roll also disappeared; various models of sleeping bag, issued according to climate and mission, are carried strapped in a thick transverse roll across the top of the pack, which is worn low. The spade moved to the left side of the belt, and the cover incorporates the bayonet scabbard. Although designated the 1956 equipment, this revised harness did not in fact appear with combat units as general issue until the early 1960s. It is still in use, and allows a good deal of flexibility in the details of the equipment carried, and in the response to climatic conditions.

93. US Marine infantryman, Korea, early 1950s

A 'leatherneck' wearing the simple and practical winter field dress issued to troops in Korea. The olive drab cap is lined with pile, and was often worn under the steel helmet with the earflaps pulled down and tied under the chin. Rank insignia were sometimes pinned to the underside of the front flap. Heavily lined over-garments and overshoes are worn over the standard field uniform; there were several models of smock and parka, often with fur-lined hoods. The light machine gun is the .30 calibre tripod-mounted Browning, the standard squad support weapon.

94. Major, US Transportation Corps, summer service dress, 1950s

An officer of the 'administrative tail' which supported the United Nations operations in Korea from the US facilities in Japan. The Major wears the light tan tropical and summer service worsted uniform and service cap, the latter with a gilt national badge and buttons and a russet leather peak and chin strap. The shirt is pale tan, with a black tie. The upper lapels carry the cut-out 'US' cypher, and the lower lapels the branch insignia; in this case the insignia comprises a small circular composite badge in the shape of a ship's steering wheel, a winged wheel and a rail. The rank is indicated by the gilt leaf of a Major pinned on the outer end of the shoulder straps. All buttons are gilt. Commissioned rank is indicated by the strip of light worsted braid around the cuffs of the tunic. The shoulder patch is that of the Japan Logistical Command. The uniform is completed by brown leather laced walking shoes.

95. Sergeant, 101st Airborne Division, early 1960s

This NCO wears the standard issue fatigue and field uniform, and is illustrated as he might appear when instructing a squad in the characteristics of the new M14 automatic rifle. The M43 fatigue cap is transformed here by 'Airborne bull' from a sloppy piece of cloth designed to keep sun and dust out of the eyes and hair, into a razor-sharp headgear suitable for an NCO in a fiercely élitist outfit. The silver parachute wings are pinned to the front.

On the point of the shoulder the white-on-blue 'AIRBORNE' title is sewn, and below it the white eagle's head on a black shield of the divisional insignia. The three chevrons of rank, in yellow on drab green, are worn on the upper arms. A name-tab, in black capitals on a white strip, is sewn above the right breast pocket, and balanced by a black strip above the left breast pocket bearing the words US ARMY; this addition to the fatigue and field uniform was introduced in the late 1950s. The collar is worn open, over a white undershirt.

The webbing belt is dark green, the normal colour for all webbing over the last decade. The high-lacing paratrooper boots are worn, with the fatigue trousers, with their two large thigh pockets, tucked into the top. Commissioned ranks wear cloth insignia of rank and branch, in the form of simple coloured duplicates of the metal insignia, sewn to the collar of the field dress – the rank badge on the wearer's right collar, the branch badge on the left.

96. Lieutenant, 3rd Infantry Regiment, 1965

The oldest regular infantry unit in the US Army – it was raised in 1784, and has a distinguished record in all its country's major wars since that date – the 3rd Infantry, or 'Old Guard', perform many ceremonial functions and have a rôle analagous to Britain's Brigade of Guards. Apart from their normal combat function they are responsible for special duties around Washington DC; they provide a colour party and a fife and drum corps dressed in the uniform of the 1780s, and a caisson party – the last mounted unit in the American forces – for state funerals. The officer illustrated, however, wears the standard green service uniform introduced in the late 1950s for all ranks of the Army, with certain parade and unit distinctions. The cut of the uniform is identical, irrespective of rank.

The service cap, with a black patent leather peak and gilt buttons, bears the gold chinstrap and gilt national insignia of an officer; non-commissioned ranks wear a black chinstrap and the national insignia embossed on a round gilt plaque rather than 'cut-out'. Infantry branch distinctions for parade wear are the pale blue shoulder cord (other branches wear cords in the relevant branch colour) and the pale blue scarf. The use of coloured scarves has been a steadily increasing practice over the last two decades. The tunic collar bears the usual gilt insignia; enlisted personnel still wear the two round embossed national and branch badges, on the upper lapel. Rank bars are pinned to the shoulder straps. Tunic buttons are gilt, for all ranks. Commissioned rank is indicated by the black worsted braid stripe around the cuffs of the tunic, and the 1½-inch stripe down the outer seam of the trousers. For normal service dress black shoes are worn, but this parade order includes black laced combat boots with the trousers tucked in. The white gloves are another parade feature.

Two particular unit distinctions are worn; the Sam Browne belt and the 'buff strap'. The black Sam Browne is worn by all ranks of the 3rd Infantry; officers wear it with the shoulder belt passing over the left shoulder, and pistol holster and magazine pouches, other ranks with the shoulder belt over the right shoulder and bayonet scabbards. The half-inch black strap worn around the left shoulder, with two lengths of quarter-inch buff leather visible to the front, recalls the Revolutionary period; the regiment is reputed to have woven strips of rawhide into the black strap of the knapsack to distinguish itself from other units.

97. Colonel of US Infantry, full dress uniform, 1960s

First adopted in the early 1950s, the full dress uniform of the US Army recalls the traditional blue of the 19th Century. This Colonel wears the dark blue peaked cap with a black cloth cover, embroidered with two arcs of gold oakleaves, fitted to the leather peak; this feature distinguishes officers of field grade. A gold chinstrap and two strips of gold braiding appear on the hat band, which is in 'infantry blue' – this varies with the branch of service. The usual gilt national insignia appears on the front of the crown. Enlisted men wear a dark blue cap with a dark blue band, irrespective of branch; the peak is black patent leather, the national insignia on a round plaque is worn on the crown, the bands of gold braiding round the top and bottom of the band are retained, and a woven golden-yellow cord chinstrap is fixed by gilt buttons.

A white shirt and black tie are visible in the open collar of the dark blue single-breasted tunic. The normal gilt national and branch insignia are pinned to the upper and lower lapels. The buttons are gilt, and full decorations are worn, as are white gloves. The blue shoulder cord of the infantry is worn on the right shoulder. Rank insignia, in the old 19th Century style, are fixed to each shoulder. A rectangle of gold braid contains an area of the branch colour, to which is fixed the metal insignia of rank – here, the eagle of a full colonel. Commissioned rank is indicated by the two strips of gold braid around the cuffs, with a central stripe in the branch colour. The trousers are pale blue for all branches, with a gold braid stripe down the outer seam.

Enlisted men wear a tunic and trousers of the same basic cut. The round insignia are pinned to the upper lapel in the usual way, and woven golden-yellow cord shoulder straps are worn. The cuffs are decorated with two gilt buttons and two lines of golden-yellow piping, and the trousers have two stripes of golden-yellow piping down the outer seam. Black shoes are worn by all ranks.

98. Private of US Airborne Cavalry, late 1960s

A soldier in the typical clothing and personal equipment of the Vietnamese War period. Despite the title of the 1st Cavalry Division (Airmobile), the unit is basically a quick-response infantry formation with its own helicopter unit under command; the personal equipment of the men is no different from that of the infantry as a whole.

The steel helmet has a faded camouflage pattern cover held in place by a rubber strap; this is more often used as a convenient carrying place for first aid kits, cigarettes, and so forth, than for the attachment of foliage. The fatigues are of a new pattern intended for jungle warfare. They are thinner, dry quicker when wetted, and have extra pockets designed to be convenient when full harness is being worn. The jungle fatigues have a relatively short life, and in the field personnel seldom bother to fix rank or unit insignia to them. Often the insignia, as in the case of the 1st Cavalry Division patch illustrated, are simply drawn straight on to the cloth of the fatigues with ballpoints or marking pens. Alternatively, various locally made versions of divisional insignia are worn, usually in dull colours. For instance, the 'subdued' version of the Cavalry Division patch for field wear is olive drab with black insignia, instead of the authorised yellow with black.

The current US webbing harness is worn, often with extra canteens; as in every army and every war, equipment is seldom worn 'by the book'. Extra magazines for the high-velocity M16 rifle are carried in cloth bandoliers. Bombs for the squad's mortar are carried in the pack, shared around the men of the section so that the burden, and the danger of losing all the ammunition with the fall of one man, is lessened. The survival knife is often worn, although it is officially issued only to flying personnel of the Division's helicopter group.

99. Patrol dress, late 1960s

The campaigns in South East Asia have produced a variety of styles of camouflage clothing, and many different patterns have been tried in the field by US forces; often these camouflage suits are not of US design but are borrowed from Vietnamese, French or other patterns. The pattern illustrated, in black, off-white, and neutral grey-green shades, is widely used. The soft bush-hat is also one of several patterns in use; American forces usually wear this type, in various finishes, while Vietnamese forces favour a wide brimmed 'Stetson' style. Insignia is only very rarely worn on camouflage clothing.

The webbing harness is the same pattern as that worn by the previous figure. A lightweight rucksack on an aluminium frame is worn on the back, with a waterproof sleeping back rolled and strapped above it; this is the 1963 Model equipment. Extra canteens and ammunition pouches are frequently carried; this soldier has improvised an extra haversack for a dozen of the 18-round magazines for the M16 rifle from a cloth bag originally used for carrying mines. A belt of ammunition for the squad's M60 machine gun is slung round his neck. His face is camouflaged with coloured greasepaint in various shades. He wears special canvas and rubber jungle boots, and the muzzle of his M16 is protected against the damp of the jungle by taping.

100. Master Sergeant (E-8) 1st Special Forces Group, late 1960s

Raised in 1952, this formation has taken on the honours and traditions of previous unconventional warfare units such as the Rangers and the Canadian-American Special Service Force of World War II. The Special Forces currently consists of ten Groups, including reserve and National Guard units. They have seen action, both clandestinely and in a conventional battlefield rôle, in many parts of the world.

The senior NCO illustrated wears the usual green service uniform of the US Army, with various unit and speciality distinctions. The forest green beret, introduced gradually since 1954 and in universal use since 1961, recalls the dress of Rogers' Rangers in the French-Indian Wars; it invites immediate comparison, of course, with the berets worn by special units of other nations – the British Royal Marine Commandos adopted a green beret in the Second World War, and the French Foreign

Legion in the mid-1950s. The cap badge is a silver device comprising crossed arrows and a sword within a scroll bearing the words 'De Oppresso Liber' – 'To Free from Oppression'. It is worn by all non-commissioned personnel, on a coloured backing patch in the shape of a shield. Officers wear normal rank insignia on the same backing patch. The colours of these patches indicate assignment, as follows: Special Forces Training Group, white: 1st SF Group, yellow, black border: 2nd SFG, teal blue, white border: 3rd SFG, segments of red, black, white, yellow: 5th SFG, black, white border, red and yellow diagonal stripes: 6th SFG, red and black, divided by white diagonal: 7th SFG, red: 8th SFG, yellow and blue divided diagonally: 10th SFG, green. The overall branch of service colour of the Special Forces is teal blue.

A smaller version of the cap device is worn pinned to the shoulder straps of the tunic by all ranks, 'inboard' of the rank markings worn by officers. Collar insignia for all ranks follows standard US Army practice; officers wear the crossed rifles of the infantry, although strictly speaking the Special Forces embrace all branches and arms. All Special Forces units have been designated as airborne formations, and on completion of a parachute qualification course personnel put up the 'AIRBORNE' shoulder title. Immediately below this on the left arm is worn the patch of the Special Forces as a whole – an arrowhead in teal blue, charged with a gold sword crossed diagonally by three gold lightning bolts. The rank chevrons and 'rockers' of a Master Sergeant are worn on both upper arms, and on the left forearm the gold 'hash marks' denote a series of four-year enlistments. The silver parachute wings on the left breast are worn on an oval backing patch in the branch colours of teal blue and gold. The tan shirt and black tie are standard; the white gloves and black boots polished to a gloss are worn for parade occasions, as in other branches of the Army.

PLATE 19

91

93

94

92

95

PLATE 20

96

97

98

99

100